I0894269

"Victoria stands with teachers, teaching assistants, care workers, family members and anyone who wishes to share fun and engaging times with and support someone with complex disabilities and neurodivergent conditions. This joyful book offers a helping hand, a pick-me-up, a message to say that you are not alone. Thumbing through the pages, you will find ideas from a whole team of contributors ready to take tired hands and say, 'Let's have some fun; let's go on a sensory adventure.' I invite you to adventure within these pages and within the spaces you may create inspired by them."

Dr Joanna Grace, *sensory engagement and inclusion specialist*

"This is a practical and empowering guide filled with easy-to-adapt ideas for creating inclusive sensory environments on any budget. Victoria brings together deep knowledge, creativity and compassion to support learners of all ages and needs. A brilliant go-to resource for educators, families and anyone looking to make a sensory difference."

Dr Sarah Moseley, *author, consultant and trainer in SEND and inclusive practice*

"An essential companion for all educators, this easy-to-use A-Z has inspiring ideas popping from every page. *Sensory Spaces* is an invaluable guide bursting with dynamic, innovative solutions. Notebook and pen ready, delve in, be excited, be enthused; create amazing sensory spaces for all your learners from the wonderful ideas. A must-have for both first-time educators entering the world of sensory learners and experienced educators seeking new inspiring ideas. The depth and breadth of this guide are phenomenal!"

Gwyn McCormack, *director, Positive Eye Ltd*

"This thoughtfully designed and accessible book would have been invaluable when I began working with children and young adults. Victoria offers a wealth of knowledge alongside innovative, sensory-rich provocations and experiences for the early years, SEND, young people and adults. A truly multi-generational resource, it empowers educators, carers and parents to foster meaningful learning through imagination, creativity and storytelling. This book is an inspiring and practical guide for anyone committed to enriching developmental experiences across all ages."

Gina Bale, *creator, Little Magic Train*

SENSORY SPACES

Imagine stepping into a sensory space where you can feel the sand between your toes, smell the sea, listen to the sound of seagulls calling; touch feathers, shells and driftwood...

Sensory spaces invite learners to be curious and try new ideas and skills, inspiring imaginative play, creativity and storytelling. This comprehensive A-Z shows readers how to create easily customisable spaces for learning, sensory engagement and relaxation, using a host of everyday items. It is packed full of:

- tools and strategies to provide positive experiences and the best outcomes for an inclusive education;
- ideas for connecting learners to different areas of the curriculum;
- sensory-rich activities to support the mental health and wellbeing of people with complex and additional needs; and
- case studies and examples from guest contributors to showcase a wide range of sensory spaces in practice.

With a rich selection of colour photographs, this essential guide will inspire you to create spaces for learners to take ownership of their sensory explorations in creative, immersive and stimulating environments. It is a valuable resource for special educational needs and disabilities (SEND) and mainstream teachers, SEND coordinators, teaching assistants, early years practitioners, play therapists, parents and carers, and anyone with an interest in engaging learners through the senses.

Victoria Navin is a passionate advocate for multisensory storytelling, specialising in creating sensory-rich learning experiences for individuals with SEND. With over two decades of experience, including working at a special school in Cheshire, she connects learners to literature, culture, history and other topics through her unique multisensory stories and sensory activities. Victoria has authored over 45 fully resourced multisensory stories and delivers online workshops for educators and caregivers worldwide. She writes sensory activities for Little Magic Train and has written sensory activities for Marvin's Storytime Show. She is a frequent speaker at online conferences and has contributed to several books (including *Sensory Stories: Making Narratives Accessible Through the Senses* by Dr Joanna Grace and *Teaching Reading to All Learners Including Those with Complex Needs* by Dr Sarah Moseley) and magazines (including *SEN Magazine* and *PMLD Link*), making her a leading figure in the field of sensory-based education.

SENSORY SPACES

AN A-Z OF IMMERSIVE AND CREATIVE ENVIRONMENTS TO SUPPORT SENSORY INTEGRATION

Victoria Navin

Routledge
Taylor & Francis Group
LONDON AND NEW YORK

Designed cover image: from top left along the top row:
Jane Mullen Speech Therapy Ltd
Christy Townson
Jennifer Abbanat

from top left along the bottom row:
Elaine Burgess
Lucy Williams
CPASS HSP Curriculum Team

First published 2026
by Routledge
4 Park Square, Milton Park, Abingdon, Oxon OX14 4RN

and by Routledge
605 Third Avenue, New York, NY 10158

Routledge is an imprint of the Taylor & Francis Group, an informa business

British Library Cataloguing-in-Publication Data
A catalogue record for this book is available from the British Library

ISBN: 9781032989143 (hbk)
ISBN: 9781032989112 (pbk)
ISBN: 9781003601364 (ebk)

DOI: 10.4324/9781003601364

Typeset in DINPro
by Deanta Global Publishing Services, Chennai, India

I dedicate this book to my late father, John Peace, whose love, kindness, integrity and wisdom continue to guide me. Your poetry ignited my passion for writing, shaping the stories I tell.

To Jacob, who sadly passed before the book was published. His memory is cherished and his legacy continues to shine in the hearts of those he touched.

To all the wonderful children and teenagers who have allowed me the privilege of sharing their sensory world. I remember each and every one of you and you will always have a special place in my heart. This book exists because of you.

TABLE OF CONTENTS

ACKNOWLEDGEMENTS

I am so lucky to work in a field surrounded by dedicated, creative and supportive people. Heartfelt thanks to everyone who contributed to this book and the children, teenagers and adults who featured in the text and photos, with or without a credit.

Thanks to Dr Joanna Grace who proofread the original and sent it to my fabulous editor, Clare.

Clare, thank you for your kindness, expertise and guidance throughout the editing process. Your support made the entire process enjoyable and I have learned so much. I couldn't have done this without you.

To Molly, the editorial assistant, thank you for your help, advice and endless patience.

My heartfelt thanks to my copyeditor, Carolyn, whose precision, insight and invaluable edits brought clarity to every page – thanks so much for your feedback, advice and guidance. Thanks to Cathy, the senior production editor, for every tweak, cut and query that got me over the finishing line—thank you for your support and calm precision in the final edits. Thank you to the production team and everyone working behind the scenes at Routledge.

Thanks to my mother, for the gift of reading and for filling my childhood with books. Thank you for encouraging my dreams and being my greatest source of wisdom and love.

Thanks to my brother Andrew, for listening to my endless ideas and proofreading my stories in those early days.

Thank you to my husband Tom, for your endless patience, support and encouragement while I was writing the book and in all that I do. You are the chapter in my life I never want to end. Your belief in me has been my greatest strength.

Thank you, reader, for buying or borrowing this book and supporting me, and for your endless hard work and dedication enhancing and enriching the lives of our sensory learners.

Finally, to all the sensory learners—you are seen, you are heard, you are cherished. Through every story and moment we share, your courage and strength open hearts and deepen understanding, teaching us how to embrace a world that feels, not just functions.

GUEST CONTRIBUTORS

Jennifer Abbanat, founder of Crow's Nest Advocacy and Consulting.

Carol Allen, educational inclusion adviser.

Tracey Allen, founder of Made for Little Feet.

The Ark Childcare, Retford.

Mary Atkinson, co-founder of the Story Massage Programme.

Gina Bale, creator and founder, Little Magic Train.

Julia Barnes, teacher at Ravenscliffe High School.

Chris Barson, founder of Positive About Autism

Peter Blaker, teacher and founder of Starfish.

Ralph Booker, autism training director (1996–2003) at the Hampshire Autistic Society.

Ryan Boren, co-founder and creative director, Stimpunks.

Rosie Brister, independent specialist.

Elaine Burgess, a senior teaching assistant and rebound therapy lead for St Giles' School.

Dr Julie Calverley, learning disability nurse and founder of NAC Wellbeing.

Lynne Castle, qualified higher-level teaching assistant at St Giles' School.

Cerebral Palsy Alliance Singapore School.

Julie Cowpe-Stephens, founder of Simply Sensory Training & Support Ltd.

Sophie Davey, SEN early years lead at Manor Green Primary School.

Debbie Delahaye, teaching assistant, and the team at Meadowfield School

Helen Dillon, founder of Simply Sensory Training & Support Ltd.

Helen Edgar, founder of Autistic Realms.

Fatemah, SEN teacher at Fairfield School.

Jo Fitzsimons, head of Flourish Specialist Educational Services.

Meiry Geraldo, founder of GALERIA AUT.

Jill Goodwin, artist and researcher.

Dr Joanna Grace, sensory engagement and inclusion specialist, researcher, author, trainer, TEDx speaker and founder of The Sensory Projects.

Claire Graham, founder of Inclusion Un.Limited.

Sarah Hall, founder of Willows Sensory Service.

Kath Hart, SEN teacher at the Beacon School.

Caroline Hill, founder of Making SENse Creative

Richard Hirstwood, director of Hirstwood Training.

Peter Imray, freelance adviser, trainer and director of developments at EQUALS.

Caroline Jacques, assistant principal for early years and the engage department at Meadowfield School.

Sophie Kidd-Munnery, parent.

Thor Kopperud, autistic artist and advocate.

Roberta Kopperud, autistic advocate.

Corinna Laurie, clinical lead occupational therapist at the National Autistic Society.

Georgie Lockett, co-creator of Songs, Signs & Sounds

Lynn McCann, specialist teacher at Reachout ASC.

Susie McClue, senior connecting families development officer at Scottish Families Affected by Alcohol and Drugs.

Gwyn McCormack, director of Positive Eye.

Jane McLean, creative director at Cheshire Dance.

Beccy Miller, complementary therapy practitioner.

Louise Mills, teacher.

Dr Sarah Moseley, author, trainer and consultant.

Emma Murphy, parent and SEN teacher.

Abi Nicholls, SEN teaching assistant.

Karen Nicholson, co-creator of Songs, Signs & Sounds.

Emma Pauley, parent and founder of People as Partners.

Chris Peak, managing director of The Apogee Project

Chelsea Pettitt.

Suzie Phillips, headteacher at Castor Church of England Primary School.

Ruth Poole, SENCO at Ellel St John's CofE Primary School.

Katie Prestage, founder of Sensory Soup.

Tigger Pritchard, speaker, trainer and consultant.

Bridget Robinson-Clark, aromatherapist and owner of See Change.

Ruth Spencer, senior lecturer/dance artist.

Moira Stephens, specialist in assistive technology, profound and multiple learning disabilities and multisensory impairment. Claremont School.

Claire Sundin, creative director at Embracing Arts.

Daniel Swift, MBE, chief executive officer and artistic director of Concrete Youth.

Christy Townson, SEN teacher at Hillside Specialist School and College.

Gerard Wainwright, learning disability nurse and founder of The Unsafe Swallow Project.

AnnMarie Walker, SEN teacher and psychotherapist.

Debby Watson, disability researcher and academic.

Amy Wells, SEN teacher at Riverside School.

Samantha Wells, owner of Poppet Tops.

Pete Wells, SEN teacher, author of Inclusive Stories for Help Kidz Learn and independent storyteller.

Joe White, deputy principal at Meadowfield School and founder of Inclusive Teach.

Lucy Williams, parent.

Pauline Woodcock, SEN teacher at Fairfield School.

Thanks are also due to the children and young adults who contributed to this book – including Aayesha, Adam Sass, Charlie Sundin, Hugh, Jacob, Liberty, Maisy, Millie, Poppy and Thomas – and all those who took part anonymously with parental permission.

Finally, many thanks to the following for their contributions and assistance:

- Helen Ashley and the team at Hebden Green School.
- Rebekah Clee.
- The Den Kit Company.
- Ellana Gilbert.
- Julie Greenall, Forest School Leader at Hillside Specialist School and College.
- Matthew Hall.
- Holly.
- The Meadowfield School Team.
- Tomoyo Nozaki, Complementary Therapist.
- Sophie and student, Ravenscliffe High School.
- Jane Mullen Speech Therapy Ltd

FOREWORD

Dr Joanna Grace

Victoria Navin has had a long career supporting people with physical and intellectual impairments and neurodivergent conditions who experience disablement. I have watched her online, through the various portholes that social media provides, try to support everyone who does jobs similar to her previous role. I know that if it were possible, she would hold every teacher's hand; guide every teaching assistant; counsel every parent; advise every portage worker, heritage worker, speech and language therapist, hospice worker, everyone ... If you are trying to support people who experience disability, then Victoria is trying to support you – and this joyful book is one of the many ways in which she is working to do this.

People such as Victoria who have a wealth of experience supporting people with complex disabilities already know the value of a sensory space. They have seen and felt it in their workplaces. They might never have considered the theory behind these spaces; there is no need when this is so tangible in practice. But it is worth taking a step back and considering where these spaces sprang from and where their value is to be found – not least so that if you are met with a puzzled expression as you attempt to erect the balloon arch that you'll find on page 27 or accessorise the sensory umbrellas on page 154, you'll be able to smooth out the frown on that face with the reassurance that you haven't lost the plot! There is a reason for the sensory rail on page 114, the peg spinner on page 104, the garden arch on page 77; and mopping up after a Shark Island adventure in the sensory room (page 121) is indeed worth it! In addition to justifying your actions to others, understanding the history of these spaces and the why behind them will help you to get the most out of the spaces you create and enable others to do the same.

The term *multisensory space* is likely to conjure mental images of a dark room lit with fibreoptics, a bubble tube glowing in the corner and perhaps interactive panels on the walls or projections on the ceiling. Multisensory rooms are technological wonderlands beloved globally. In the UK, all special schools are expected to have them (Department for Education 2015) – and many schools have more than one. We also find them in adult care settings, hospitals, airports, even football stadiums. They can cost a small (or not so small) fortune. Perhaps you picked up this book because you wanted one but could not afford it, and you are considering an improvised sensory space as a second-best to these more apparently impressive spaces. But remember: the original multisensory rooms were tents, cardboard boxes, improvised spaces – just like the ones you will find in the pages of this book. The inspiration behind their creation came from deep personal relationships, love, connection and friendship, with one human desiring to create a space in which another human could rest with them and find joy.

Jan Hulsegge and Ad Verheul are widely regarded as the pioneers of the multisensory rooms we know today. In the late 1970s, they set up a tent in the grounds of the De Hartenberg Centre in the Netherlands with the aim of enabling some of the centre's more profoundly disabled residents to participate in the summer fair. Combining their love of nature with their understanding and care for the residents of De Hartenberg, whom they viewed as friends, they brought into the tent natural experiences that they hoped the residents would enjoy. The tent was envisaged as a protective place which would provide the sensory backdrop that these people needed in order to be able to perceive the natural materials (fragrant flowers, crunchy leaves, springy branches) offered to them. The reactions of the people sharing that space were so pronounced that the institution allocated a room inside the building for the pair to continue the practice that they called '*Snozelen*'. Jan and Ad describe *Snozelen* as a process of attuning to another person and sharing experience (Hulsegge and Verheul 1988) – a description that many today would understand as 'intensive interaction' (Nind and Hewett 1994). Their focus was on valuing the other person and sharing experiences of value. The room that they created in the De Hartenberg Centre was the first multisensory room and word of the remarkable things that were happening there spread far and wide. People came to visit to witness the practice of *Snozelen*, and Jan and Ad worked hard to facilitate understanding around the world so that similar experiences could be enjoyed elsewhere.

Great ideas often spring up several times before the time is right for them to take root. That Jan and Ad's tent was so successful is a testament both to their inventiveness and to the willingness of people in the late 1970s and early 1980s to view those with intellectual and physical impairments differently, focusing less on their impairments and more on their capacities. It was during this period that the social model of disability was developed by disability activists. The challenge to the medical model of disability provided by the social model is reflected in narratives from the time that describe sensory rooms as enabling spaces. No longer do we view disability as located *in* a person; instead, we see it as occurring *between* a person and their environment. Suddenly we are more attentive to the spaces around people, where space = place + relationships within that place. Creating a place in which relationships can flourish is key to sensory room practice and to creating valuable improvised sensory spaces. This understanding of the importance of environment is seen in Dr Lilli Neilson's Little Rooms (1988), in which responsive materials are hung from a frame so that they dangle within reach of the person lying beneath the frame: moving a leg or waving an arm will be rewarded by the sound of a bell ringing or the glittering of a reflective ball twirling. Lilli's work is reflected in the improvised sensory spaces that Flo Longhorn (1988) created out of giant cardboard boxes (the boxes that washing machines – or even motorbikes! – come in). Jan and Ad's work is echoed in her emptying cupboards of their contents, painting them black to provide a plain visual backdrop and resourcing them with UV torches and glowing items to create spaces in which to provide cortically visually impaired children with visual stimulation programmes to support their development. Les Staves and Keith Park (in his fabulously titled 'Loitering Within Tent' article) both sing the praises of a simple tent and torch approach to sensory spaces:

> Remotely generated effects of lights, or sharks, or thunderstorms sweeping across the ceiling are impressive and exciting, but they should not devalue the fun of playing with a torch under a sheet or in a tent where the source of the fun can both be understood and affected.
>
> *(Staves 2018, personal communication)*

> With a blanket over the tent to give a dark interior, and a pen torch to illuminate the material, the effect was similar to Greenwich Planetarium – as well as being cheaper and quieter!
>
> *(Park 1997)*

Improvised spaces and the relationships within them have always been championed through the history of multisensory room practice. The significance of relationships within a place resonates through the work of Jean Ware (2012), which speaks of the importance of responding to the embodied communication of people with complex disabilities. What we learn from these pioneers of sensory practice who have travelled this road before us is that the magic of sensory spaces is created from a combination of environment and relationships within that environment. That magic is as possible to achieve within environments built from things that other people might pop in their recycling bins as it is within environments that cost thousands upon thousands of pounds.

Hirstwood and Gray (1995) were among the first witnesses of early sensory room practice and their statement that 'The stressed are relaxing, the silent are speaking, and the withdrawn are coming out of themselves' speaks to the transformative nature of those first sensory room experiences. Barbara McCormack (2003) recalls taking her daughter Sarah into a multisensory room for the first time. Up until then, Sarah had, in Barabara's words:

> Communicated her basic needs with tears ranging from blood curdling screams when myoclonic jerks terrified her to heart-rending, inconsolable sobs that lasted hours. That was it – nothing else. No hints that she belonged to the world or wanted to be here. No recognition, nor gurgles ... and certainly no giggles.
>
> *McCormack (2003:38)*

But in the sensory room, her daughter smiled and squealed with delight, kicked her legs and engaged her senses with the room: 'for the first time my daughter wanted to be a part of the world!' (McCormack 2003:38) That space was a connection point for them, a way of finding each other, sharing time and experience; and this is what sensory spaces remain for many people today.

Initially the proliferation of sensory rooms that occurred in the late 1980s and early 1990s was a passion project driven by those who had witnessed their power and wanted to share it with others. It is notable that many who began this work in the 1970s and 1980s continue it to this day, such is their missionary zeal for the project. But as the rooms took off and became commercially successful, people began to be motivated by financial opportunity rather than the transformative potential of these spaces. (This link between the commercial potential of sensory rooms and their increased uptake is observed by researchers such as Mount and Cavet (1995), Pagliano (2001) and Botts et al (2008).) Eavesdropping on the sector today, you are as likely to hear salespeople bragging about units sold as you are conversations about lives changed. The technological advances that we have seen in recent years have continued to fuel the boom in profits and researchers whose work touches on these spaces have voiced concerns that change is being driven by technological capacity rather than potential impact (Challis et al 2017; Grace 2019).

Fowler (2008) reports anecdotal research evidence suggesting that multisensory rooms can help people to relax; reduce challenging behaviour, agitation and anxiety; enhance interaction between people and the environment; and increase concentration. There has always been a ready supply of such evidence on the power of multisensory spaces; but as the desire for profits eclipsed the need for connection, it has become more common for people to begin designing their spaces by thumbing the pages of a catalogue or responding to a tantalising ad than by considering their relationships with those with whom they hope to share the spaces. As the costs of commercial spaces escalate, researchers have increasingly questioned whether they offer value for money (Ayer 1998; Lancioni et al 2002; Haegele and Porretta 2014; Grace 2019). This scepticism is not meant as a rebuttal of the anecdotal evidence that flows so readily from spaces created from relationships and connection; rather, it reflects an awareness that when budgets are limited, commercially installed rooms do not necessarily represent value for money. The call is for consideration:

'Is this really what you want, what you need? What is best for the person you are seeking to support?'

In 2018, I undertook research into the use of multisensory rooms in the UK, identifying the characteristics of effective sensory rooms and the barriers to effective practice within them (Grace 2020, 2021). You can read about this research in detail in *Multiple Multisensory Rooms: Myth Busting the Magic* (Grace 2019), together with a more in-depth history of sensory rooms and the philosophy surrounding them than that which I have given here; but for the purposes of this book, the three main findings from that research are particularly pertinent. I discovered that what set effective sensory rooms apart from those deemed to be less effective was not particular pieces of equipment; it was not whether the setting in question had the latest gadget or whether one sensory room was as good as the sensory room at the school in the neighbouring town. Rather, what practitioners in the spaces attributed their power to was: (1) that they were novel spaces; (2) that they were spaces in which light could be controlled; and (3) that the people using the spaces were not interrupted. The novelty of the space gave freedom: this space was not a classroom in which a particular set of behaviours was expected, or a dinner hall, a living room, a bedroom. These places already have attached to them a particular set of actions and behaviours that are expected within them. The provision of a novel space was an offer of freedom; it was saying at an environmental level: 'Here there are no pre-set rules – you can decide who and how you want to be here.' I am reminded as I write of Flo Longhorn's first formally installed sensory room in the school she presided over, which she called 'the Rumpus room':

> It cost about £2,000, funded by local pubs. Two men from Wales came and slept in the school hall and feasted on school dinners as they built it. I designed it around the children. It had a copy of the book *Where the Wild Things Are* hung on the door to remind staff that there were no rules in the room. The children were liberated from the tyranny of adults hovering and supervising them through the use of a stable door.
>
> *(Longhorn 2018)*

Her intent was that within that room, the children would be free to be exactly as they wanted to be; to run wild if they wanted to; to start a rumpus!

The finding relating to light speaks to the visual impairment or visual processing differences experienced by the population of people being offered time in multisensory spaces. The ability to dim the lights, to control the visual stimulus within the room, enables the person facilitating in the space to balance the environment to the visual capacities of the person sharing it. Visually more cluttered spaces or spaces which require the processing of an enormous amount of light place more demands on those within them, which can equate to less access, less ability, more stress, more disablement. As you choose and create your improvised sensory space, considering the light levels and how you can adjust the visual stimulus within it will be key to the success of sharing that space with people.

Finally, avoiding the risk of interruption speaks to these being places about relationships. The sensory space is somewhere to be together, to feel together, to sense together. Nothing is added to that time by your phone going off or someone sticking their head around the door to deliver a message. Jill Goodwin's doctoral research (2019) adds depth to this idea of sensory spaces serving as a place of refuge from the day-to-day pressures of life. This was extended in her postdoctoral work with Oily Cart, *'Being With' in Sensory Theatre* (Goodwin and Griffith 2022), which supported the development of a bespoke theatre experience posted to families during the COVID-19 lockdowns in the UK in 2020. 'Space to Be' provided families with an improvised sensory space that they could create at home, in which they could escape the pressures of life and indulge in beautiful sensory experiences. The most powerful sensory spaces are spaces made for relationships and connection supported by, but not demanding, an engagement with the sensory world.

My research involved interviewing people who used sensory rooms about their experiences of using them. During our conversations, I would often ask them whether a novel space in which they had control over the lighting and no one interrupted them might be more useful to them than the sensory room we were talking about. The answer was always a hearty and hopeful 'yes' – not because there was anything necessarily wrong with the rooms we were discussing, but because of all the barriers to effective practice that people experienced in relation to those rooms. These barriers included timetable clashes, the room being far away, the need to make choices as to who could access the room or a fee charged to enter a room. My suggested improvised space came without any of these barriers and was thus immediately appealing. The people whom I interviewed understood that the value of a sensory space is not to be found in its price tag but in the relationships that are possible within it.

And so it is that, throughout a history of more than 50 years, it has often been the case that the best sensory spaces are the improvised ones we make ourselves; the homemade ones; the ones that do not look as impressive as those in the catalogues, but which have placed particular people at their heart from their inception. Challis (2014:216) advises that 'acknowledging the effectiveness of ad-hoc, small-scale spaces built around the needs of the individual and gently moving away from the generic commercial resource may well be the way forward'. The value of a sensory space is not to be found in fancy materials or high-tech equipment, but in the relationships made possible by the protection of the space. Personalised spaces that give people permission to play and to be together. Spaces without pressure. Spaces that protect you from the world outside. Spaces of liberation and sensory adventure.

The people who created the original multisensory rooms started not by flicking through catalogues of bubble tubes and fibreoptics, but by thinking about the people they supported and inventing spaces for them. As you flick through the pages of this book, hold the person you wish to share the space with at heart and think of what would be best for them. Maybe you won't make any of these spaces but instead will be inspired to create one of your very own: Victoria and I would love to hear from you if you do!

(You can see images of more improvised sensory spaces at www.facebook.com/media/set/?set=a.741268032940594&type=3 – you are a part of the rich history of improvised sensory spaces now!)

References

Ayer, S (1998). Use of multi-sensory rooms for children with profound and multiple learning disabilities. *Journal of Learning Disabilities*, 2(2), 89-97. https://doi.org/10.1177/146900479800200206

Botts, BH, Hershfeldt, PA, Christen-Sandfort, RJ & Snoezelen (2008). Empirical review of product representation. *Focus on Autism and Other Developmental Disabilities*, 23(3), 138-47.

Challis, B (2014) Designing for Musical Play. Manchester Metropolitan University.

Challis, B, Kang, A, Rimmer, R & Hildred, M (2017). Enabling active interaction with music and sound in multisensory environments. *EAI Endorsed Transactions on Creative Technologies*, 4(11), 153060. https://doi.org/10.4108/eai.5-9-2017.153060

Department for Education (2015) Area guidelines for SEND and alternative provision. Building Bulletin 104. https://assets.publishing.service.gov.uk/media/5f23ec4e8fa8f57ac968fb11/BB104.pdf

Department for Education and Department of Health and Social Care (2024). SEND code of practice: 0 to 25 years. https://www.gov.uk/government/publications/send-code-of-practice-0-to-25

Fowler, S (2008). Multisensory rooms and environments. Controlled Sensory Experiences for People with Profound and Multiple Disabilities. JKP Resource Materials.

Goodwin, J (2019). Sharing an Aesthetic Space of Refuge Within a School for Pupils with Profound and Multiple Learning Disabilities: Golden Tent [PhD Thesis, University of Winchester]. https://winchester.elsevierpure.com/en/studentTheses/sharing-an-aesthetic-space-of-refuge-within-a-school-for-pupils-w

Goodwin, J & Griffiths, E (2022). 'Being With' in Sensory Theatre. Routledge.

Goodwin, M (2013). Listening and responding to children with PMLD – towards a framework and possibilities. *The SLD Experience*, 65(1), 21-27. https://www.ingentaconnect.com/contentone/bild/sld/2013/00000065/00000001/art00005

Grace, J (2020a). Multiple Multisensory Rooms: Myth Busting the Magic. Routledge.

Grace, J (2020b). Multisensory rooms: Essential characteristics and barriers to effective practice. *Tizard Learning Disability Review*, 25(2). https://doi.org/10.1108/TLDR-10-2019-0029

Grace, J (2021). Get it? *PMLD Link*, 33(1) 98, 27-28.

Haegele, JA & Porretta, DL (2014). Snoezelen multisensory environment: An overview of research and practical implications. *Palaestra*, 28(4), 29-33.

Hirstwood, R & Gray, M (1995). A Practical Guide to the Use of Multi-Sensory Rooms. Toys for the Handicapped.

Hulsegge, J & Verheul, A (1987). Snoezelen: Another World. Rompa.

Lancioni, GE, Cuvo, AJ & O'Reilly, MF (2002) Snoezelen: An overview of research with people with developmental disabilities and dementia. *Disability and Rehabilitation*, 24(4), 175-184.

Longhorn, F (1984). Planning a Sensory Curriculum and Sensory Banks for the Very Special Child: A Practical Approach to Curriculum Planning. Souvenir Press.

Longhorn, F (2018) Personal communication with the author.

McCormack, B. (2003). Snoezelen: A mother's story. *The Exceptional Parent*, 22(10), 38-41.

Mount, H & Cavet, J (1995). Multi-sensory environments: An exploration of their potential for young people with profound and multiple learning disabilities. *British Journal of Special Education*, 22(2), 52-55.

Neilson, L (1988). Spatial Relations in Chronically Blind Infants – thesis. National Institute for Blind and Partially Sighted Children and Youth.

Nielsen, L (1992). Space and Self: Active Learning by Means of the Little Room. SIKON.

Nind, M & Hewett, D (1994). Access to Communication: Developing Basic Communication with People Who Have Severe Learning Difficulties (Second Edition). David Fulton Publishers.

Pagliano, P (2001). Using a Multi Sensory Environment – A Practical Guide for Teachers. David Fulton Publishers

Ware, J (2012). Creating a Responsive Environment for People with Profound and Multiple Learning Difficulties. Routledge. https://doi.org/10.4324/9780203065266

ABOUT THIS BOOK

Imagine stepping into a sensory space where you can feel the sand between your toes; smell the sea; hear seagulls calling; touch feathers, shells, seaweed, driftwood; and taste ice cream. Or imagine embracing a tranquil space bathed in soothing music, with snug blankets and cushions and different scents and textures for you to explore and express your sensory preferences, making choices and rejections within a safe and therapeutic environment.

This resource will guide on you how to create easily customisable working spaces and immersive environments, inviting curiosity and providing sensory feedback using arches, cardboard boxes, curtains, hula hoops, parachutes, parasols, rails, tents, umbrellas and a host of other everyday items. A place for sensory space users to try out new ideas and skills; to take ownership of their playtime and explorations; to feel inspired through imaginative play, creativity and storytelling; and to make decisions about how they want to spend their time.

People with complex and additional needs require unique support. The shift towards greater awareness, inclusivity and individualised learning is shaping the way we support people, leading to growing demand for resources to help those working in education and the adult care sector, as well as parents, carers, family and friends, to provide the best support to meet their sensory needs.

Early years practitioners and childminders, professionals in special educational needs and disabilities and mainstream schools and colleges will find ideas, tools and strategies to help their students gain a positive and full experience and optimal outcomes from an inclusive education, and suggestions and activities to connect learners to areas of the curriculum – including the arts, literature, culture, history and other topics – through the senses.

Support workers, carers and activity coordinators can also integrate these ideas to aid delivery of sensory-rich activities to support the mental health and wellbeing of people with complex and additional needs and adults with dementia within their home, day centre or care setting.

The book is cross-generational and its grab-and-go, easy-to-follow format makes the content accessible for parents, grandparents, sons, daughters, siblings and friends.

With case studies, photos and features of sensory spaces in practice, creative ideas to inspire you and insights and ideas from professionals working in the education field, inclusion specialists, parents and sensory space users themselves, you will gain confidence in setting up creative, immersive and stimulating environments for use in early years provisions, classrooms, daycare centres, residential settings or in the home.

Wherever possible, I have chosen environmentally sustainable, recycled or reusable resources that don't harm the environment.

HOW TO USE THIS BOOK

The opening parts of this book provide an overview of sensory processing and the different sensory profiles that individuals may have. They explore the advantages of using sensory structures and spaces; offer guidance on ownership of space; provide insights on selecting and accessorising sensory spaces; and address safety considerations.

The following sections are organised in an A-Z format, showcasing items used to create sensory spaces with in-practice evidence and photographs demonstrating the concepts in action, their context and outcomes to support you in advocating for the implementation of such spaces in your own setting.

The concluding parts of the book tie together the insights and concepts explored in the book with ideas aligned with the needs of specific demographic groups, guiding you on how to put these into practice within your home, classroom or other setting, with examples of zones and activities linked to the individual senses, activities or a specific topic or theme.

Navigate the book at your own pace, dipping in and out of the A-Z for inspiration. Read guest contributions for a different perspective; explore creating your own sensory spaces with inspiration from the 'Zones' section; or find links to more information in the 'Further Resources' section.

Part 1

INTRODUCING SENSORY SPACES

DOI: 10.4324/9781003601364-1

Sensory Processing

'Sensory processing' refers to the way our brains receive, interpret and respond to information from our environment.

There are eight main sensory systems in our body which provide information about the world around us.

Sight: Sight delivers visual information about our surroundings. Our eyes detect colour, light, movement and shapes. Stimulate the visual system by presenting familiar and new stimuli. Incorporate bright, bold colours and textures using contrasting backgrounds in visual materials to capture attention. Explore different light sources – fibreoptic lights, finger lights, glow-in-the dark/UV objects and torches – to create stimulating visual experiences. Introduce movement using bubbles, bubble tubes, hanging mobiles, interactive screens, light projectors, mobiles, sensory bottles, wind-spinners or swinging objects to enhance visual tracking.

Hearing: Our sense of hearing informs us about our environment, aids communication, enables us to enjoy music and alerts us to danger. When an object vibrates, the sound it creates travels through the air to our ear canals as sound waves, causing the eardrum to vibrate. These vibrations are amplified by inner ear bones and converted into electrical signals which are sent to the brain through the auditory nerve. The brain processes these signals, enabling us to perceive and interpret sounds.

Stimulate the auditory system through music, sound effects, interactive books and sound toys, singing, storytelling, talking and humming, sound discrimination activities and nature walks.

Smell: Closely linked to the sense of taste, receptors in the nose send chemicals detected in the air to our brains, helping us identify them and navigate the world around us and keeping us safe (eg, the smell of smoke or spoilt food alerts us to potential danger). The sense of smell is closely linked to memory and can evoke emotions – for example, a specific perfume may remind us of a person. Different smells affect us in different ways. We can bring this into our practice using scents to create and change our environment.

Enhance olfactory stimulation using aromatherapy oils, cooking and baking, diffusers, massage with scented creams, scented objects, herbs and flowers. Add scent to mouldables and paints; spritz onto scarves or cushions; explore scented sensory bags; and incorporate smells into storytelling.

Touch: Receptors in the skin respond to stimuli, providing information about the pressure, texture and qualities of physical items (eg, bristly, bumpy, fluffy), enhancing our sensory experiences and facilitating our understanding of the environment. Through touch, we experience emotion and can protect ourselves from danger (eg, if something is hot or sharp).

Promote tactile engagement through art and crafts, gardening, massage – offer a choice of body brushes, mitts and rollers. Explore textured fabrics and materials, sand and water play, sensory bins, boxes and trays, sensory play using Oobleck and Playdoh®, tactile books and sensory boards.

Taste: The sense of taste enables us to distinguish different flavours and textures in the food we eat. Tastebuds located on the tongue and in the mouth send signals to the brain, which processes and interprets the information to determine whether a food is sweet, sour, salty, bitter or umami (savoury). These basic groups can be explored further (eg, citrus, floral, fruity, herbal).

Introduce, bake, cook, explore and sample a range of fruits, vegetables, dips, herbal teas and international cuisines. Play blindfold tasting games; introduce new foods; experiment with flavour combinations; make food art (eg, fruit kebabs, pizza faces, shaped sandwiches); explore food at different temperatures (frozen, warm); infuse water with fruit; make smoothies, milkshakes and soups; taste herbs and spices; and grow your own produce.

Vestibular: This system provides us with information about where our body is in the space around us, direction of movement and speed.

Climbing, dancing, jumping, hopping, riding, rocking, rolling, skipping, sliding, spinning, swinging, twirling and practising yoga are all activities which can help improve balance, coordination and overall vestibular function.

Proprioception: This system provides us with information about where a body part is and how it is moving.

Activities to engage the muscles and joints to improve coordination, proprioception and overall body awareness include balancing, bouncing, catching and throwing, carrying objects (backpacks), crawling, heavy work (pushing, pulling, rolling and lifting), navigating obstacle courses, squeezing, stacking, swimming, working with resistance bands and wearing compression clothing.

Interoception: This system provides us with information on how our body is feeling and our internal body sensations (eg, anxious, hungry, tired).

Activities to help people tune into their interoception include belly breathing, body awareness games ('Simon Says'), body scans, emotional mapping (identify and label where feelings and sensations arise from), gentle stretching, guided relaxation, heartbeat awareness, increasing hydration, mindfulness breathing, eating, colouring, walking, pilates, tai chi, and yoga.

Please consider health and safety and consult with the person's physiotherapist or occupational therapist if you are uncertain about any of these activities.

Sensory Profiles

A 'sensory profile' describes how individuals process and react to sensory input from the environment using information from our senses.

There are three main categories that make up a person's sensory profile:

- A **sensory seeker** pursues strong sensory input – such as intense smells, physical pressure, loud music – to feel balanced and organised.
- A **sensory avoider** may actively limit their exposure to sensory stimuli (eg, 'too loud', 'too bright', 'too busy').
- For **sensory sensitive** people, their heightened response to sensory stimuli may cause discomfort.

All three sensory profiles can impact communication and interaction.

By identifying a person's sensory profile, we can better understand how they respond to sensory stimuli and interact with the environment, helping us to support them. Writing a sensory plan incorporating tailored activities and strategies to aid the person (eg, providing movement breaks for a sensory seeker or establishing a calm environment for someone who is sensory avoidant) promotes wellbeing and fosters positive outcomes.

This book will help you to create sensory environments to support individuals with different sensory profiles.

The Benefits of Using Sensory Structures and Sensory Spaces

A 'sensory space' is a customisable area or zone containing elements tailored to meet individual's needs sensory needs. These spaces offer numerous benefits:

- **Enriched learning experiences:** By creating immersive themed learning spaces to connect learners to literacy, culture, history and other topics, you can bring lessons to life as your space transforms into an art studio, rainforest or science lab.
- **Development of social and emotional skills:** By sharing a space, sensory space users can build social interactions, practising social skills, turn-taking and listening to others' ideas.
- **Imaginative play and storytelling:** The imagination is the only limit as a sensory space transforms into a spaceship, castle, shop, boat or seaside.
- **Greater independence, confidence and responsibility:** These are all promoted as individuals learn new skills through setting up and personalising a sensory space and making decisions about their activities, explorations and how they spend their time in the space.
- **A safe and therapeutic setting:** Sensory spaces afford a safe and therapeutic setting in which individuals can explore sensory development or to which they can retreat for regulation.
- **Versatile indoor and outdoor fun:** Sensory spaces can be set up indoors or outdoors.

Ownership of Sensory Spaces

Several steps can be taken to address the risk of 'ownership' of sensory spaces – the potential conflict that can arise when someone becomes territorial about a space or resource and experiences difficulty in sharing and turn-taking, particularly in group settings such as classrooms or playgroups:

- Establish clear rules and boundaries regarding usage.
- Model and encourage sharing and cooperative play.
- Use timers, designated time slots and breakaway groups to help individuals learn to share spaces, take turns and practise waiting – all essential life skills.

A space can be used as both a shared and personal area. One pre-school that I worked in had a pop-up 'birthday tent' that a child could customise for the afternoon.

Suzie Phillips, headteacher at **Castor Church of England Primary School**, shares her thoughts on ownership of a shared space.

Ownership of Sensory Spaces

Suzie Phillips

In early years foundation stage (EYFS), the reading nook (see page 106) serves as an integral communal space where children learn to navigate sharing and cooperation. From the moment they enter EYFS, children are taught that the space accommodates a maximum of four individuals at any given time. This protocol ensures that children do not feel overcrowded and promotes more focused engagement with the activities available. The reading nook is not strictly timetabled; rather, children are encouraged to enter the space freely but within the established guidelines. When one child leaves, another can enter, fostering a continuous flow that allows for sustained interaction without disruption.

In this thoughtfully curated environment, children participate in various activities, including reading games, engaging in roleplay, retelling stories and applying sounds that they have learned to construct words from books.

Additionally, they have the opportunity to listen to stories on CDs, unimpeded by interruptions. Such provisions enable all children to access the reading nook throughout the day, promoting a culture of shared learning and exploration.

The books held within the nook are meticulously aligned with the curriculum and have already been introduced to the children, ensuring familiarity and encouraging a deeper literary engagement. This strategic approach assists in nurturing a love for reading while promoting collaborative play.

Part 2
GETTING STARTED

DOI: 10.4324/9781003601364-2

Health and Safety Guidance

Please read before engaging in the activities.

Tents and sensory spaces are intended to be sensory areas, immersive environments – places of retreat, relaxation and socialisation. Tents must not be zipped fully closed from the outside or used as a restraint – individuals should be free to enter and leave as they wish. A sensory space should NEVER be used as a form of isolation or a form of discipline.

Ensure all activities comply with your school or setting safeguarding policies.

- The author has used their best efforts in preparing the information in this book and makes no representation or warranties with respect to the accuracy, applicability, fitness or completeness of the contents.
- If you choose to implement any ideas or activities from this resource, you take full responsibility for your actions.
- The activities are designed to be led and supervised by a responsible adult at all times.
- Ensure your sensory structures are secured safely, with no sharp ends or tripping hazards.
- Be aware of potential suffocation or choking hazards in all props, materials and accessories used.
- Interactions should be led by the sensory explorer, who should participate without expectation.
- If you have any doubts regarding any activity, material or accessory used, please seek advice before starting.

Allergies/Intolerances

- Never force stimuli and stop the activity if the sensory explorer shows signs that they are not enjoying the activity or stimuli.
- Check the ingredients in any items that you may be using for potential food or skin allergies or respiratory reactions. If you see any signs of redness, swelling or other symptoms of a suspected reaction, seek immediate medical advice.

Using Scents and Smells

Some individuals may have heightened sensitivity to scents and smells, so exercise caution when using them to ensure the person's comfort and wellbeing. Offer choices and be mindful of individual preferences: some people may prefer strong scents, while others may prefer subtle ones. If the space is being used by multiple people, ensure everyone likes the scents you are using. Whenever possible, use natural materials – herbs and spices and essential oils – rather than synthetic products. When introducing a new scent, test it out in a small amount. Magnetic spice jars are excellent containers: their clear lid enables you to see the contents, and the pour and sprinkle openings allow control over how much scent is released.

Jo Fitzsimons is head of **Flourish Specialist Education Services**. Her doctoral thesis on smell revealed lots of interesting insights into how the effective use of smell can support learning.

Practical Strategies for the Presentation and Use of Smells to Support Learning

Jo Fitzsimons

- Use smells routinely as part of a multisensory activity.
- Tell the person what smell you are going to offer them.
- Gently touch or stroke the person's nose as a cue to smelling if they cannot bring a scented item to their own nose.
- Be sensitive to the person's responses.
- Be aware of any other environmental factors, such as noise or talking, that may affect the person's responses to smell.
- Look out for changes in mouth and tongue movement in response to smell.
- Allow the person to taste or lick scented items if they wish do so and if it is safe for them.
- If you are offering food to a person who needs support with eating and drinking, offer its smell first and then wait for their response before bringing it to their lips.
- If the person cannot consume food items, lip swipe if it is allowed.
- Allow the person to touch and explore scented items with their hands or feet.
- Ensure the person is interested and able to engage with any containers that you use.

- If the person is unable to hold and bring scented items to their nose, gradually bring the smell to their nose from a distance until they appear to detect and are comfortable with it.
- Hold the smell in a position that is comfortable and allow the person to experience it for extended periods of time if they show signs of pleasure.
- Withdraw a smell if a person shows signs of displeasure or that they have had enough of the smelling activity.

Choosing a Sensory Structure or Space

Space and budget are likely to be the two most important factors when choosing a sensory structure. Consider the following:

- **Accessibility:** Ensure easy access, enabling obstacle-free entry and exit.
- **Activity level in the immediate environment:** Opt for a quiet location with minimum distractions. Avoid placing your sensory structure next to a door, an area with high people traffic or a frequently accessed cupboard.
- **Comfort:** Position away from a draughty window, fan, heater or direct sunlight.
- **Cost:** This resource contains ideas for sensory structures that you can buy and budget-friendly options that can be made using everyday materials.
- **Flexibility:** Will the space be temporary space (eg, for one lesson/session) or a more permanent feature (eg, a theme for half a term)?
- **Lighting:** Adapt the lighting to suit the purpose of your space – soft lighting for a relaxing space; light via a colour-changing lamp to create an immersive environment (eg, blue for the ocean or natural light for arts, crafts and puzzles).
- **Noise level:** To minimise noise, lay down a thick rug, add cushions or use background music and sounds.
- **Person:** Who will be using the space? Consider any physical and/or sensory needs that need supporting.
- **Purpose:** Is the sensory space a place for relaxation, reading, sensory exploration or play; or an immersive space for education?
- **Safety:** Place your tent away from potential hazards and find a balance between privacy and a space where sensory space users can be supervised.
- **Storage:** Incorporate storage into your sensory space using bags, baskets, boxes, nets and shoe hangers.

Helen Edgar, founder of **Autistic Realms**, and **Ryan Boren**, who helped to start **Stimpunks**, discuss niche construction – how each person's and each group's sensory space will look and feel different based upon their needs.

Niche Construction

Helen Edgar and Ryan Boren

It is essential to consider how sensory differences, physical impairments and medical needs may impact people's learning experiences and the importance of adopting a neurodiversity-affirming, strengths-based approach when setting up personalised learning environments, being open and flexible to changes that will be needed.

Consider each individual person's:

- access to resources;
- communication aids;
- health and wellbeing;
- likes and interests;
- multisensory profile; and
- positioning and comfort.

The founder of **Inclusive Teach** and deputy principal at **Meadowfield School** in Kent, **Joe White** is a parent to two autistic children. Joe has a wealth of experience and insight into the challenges and triumphs faced by individuals with diverse learning requirements. Here, Joe shares his top tips on engaging students in sensory experiences.

Engaging Students in Sensory Experiences

Joe White

- **Don't overwhelm the individual with resources:** Introduce new elements gradually so students can explore each one rather than always heading for a favourite. If you have a box or bag, remove one item at a time; if you are using a sensory room, cover some elements with a plain black sheet.
- **Provide choice and control:** Allow the student choice and control to make the experience as positive as possible and provide a clear way to say 'no' or 'stop'. If the student does not have a communication system, add symbols or resources to the room.
- **Gradate sensory experiences:** The transition from bright corridor lights to a darker sensory room can create a barrier for the individual to process. Likewise, turning the lights on at the end of a session can be jarring. Slowly increase/decrease light and sound levels.

- **Create a sensory biography:** Make the experience meaningful to the individual. A sensory biography could include dad's aftershave or the texture of mum's favourite scarf. This can increase the feeling of safety and reduce anxiety.
- **Theme your space:** Increase interest and engagement by theming your space to individuals or topics. Use coloured lights and background 'ambience' sounds on YouTube to create immersive jungles or underwater experiences. These spaces are great to read a book in.

Accessorising Sensory Spaces

The aim of accessorising a sensory space is to make it inviting and functional. There are endless possibilities for creating zones that people enjoy spending time in. The layout may also depend on individual needs and preferences, so involve the sensory space user(s) in setting up the space and choosing accessories to create a personalised and effective sensory experience. Some people may prefer a minimalist environment with fewer items; others a more sensory-rich environment with a variety of stimulating items.

Ideas for accessorising a sensory space include the following:

- **Colour and texture:** Add patterned and plain carpet tiles, rugs, throws, blankets, beanbags, fabric and material swatches, wall hangings, glow in the dark stickers, glitter/lava lamps and tactile boards.
- **Decorate with artwork:** Using the person's artwork or chosen artwork adds a personal touch.
- **Educational elements:** Decorate with posters, maps, information, facts or educational charts; set up storytelling corners; provide hands-on activities and sensory learning stations.
- **Engage the senses:** Choose items to engage the five main senses or focus on one sense at a time.
- **Introduce light:** String fairy lights (secure the battery) around the perimeter or ceiling of your structure; hang mobiles and objects that reflect and refract light; use mini projectors; offer the use of torches and light toys and accessories.
- **Provide entertainment:** This could include books, activities, games, toys and visual/audio equipment (eg, an iPad) for listening to music or audiobooks. Promote literacy skills by labelling the boxes/bags/baskets in which the items are stored.
- **Provide seating options:** These could include cushions, beanbags and carpet mats of different textures, chairs, a hammock, a pressure therapy chair or a sleeping bag.
- **Smell:** Modify the atmosphere using oil diffusers, herbs and scented plants; or spritz scents onto fabric.
- **Sound:** Use sound buttons; play music; provide musical instruments and items that make interesting sounds.
- **Theme:** Accessorise to a topic or theme (see Part 5: Sensory Zones on page 185 for ideas and inspiration).

Before we move on to the A-Z of sensory structures, here are some overarching ideas from practitioners to think about when planning and using sensory spaces.

Claire Sundin – creative director at **Embracing Arts**, a theatre company dedicated to creating multisensory, interactive, experiences for children with special educational needs and disabilities (SEND) – shares her ideas on creating a sensory atmosphere.

Creating a Sensory Atmosphere

Claire Sundin

At Embracing Arts, we often visit many different classrooms in a day and creating a sensory space within those areas (in a short period of time – there is usually very little set-up time for us!) can be challenging. However, there are many positives of being in a familiar environment to the group, as the space is 'safe' to them, so there is one less variable to consider (bearing in mind that we – the facilitators – can often be new to the pupils, their routine has been disrupted and we are bringing in new sensory stimuli).

We use the following to create the sensory atmosphere:

- **Music:** Usually something instrumental and calming, and a welcome song to introduce ourselves and find out the names of group members.
- **Sheets:** Lots of different textures. I particularly like using sheer fabrics which you can see through, keeping an eye on your safe space, but which can also be wafted/explored, pulled and twisted.
- **Lighting:** Always a fun one – often the battle begins between students who prefer the lights off and those who like them on. If we are unable to change the lighting state, we use transparent umbrellas lined with colourful fairy lights, placing a dark material or blanket over the top for those who want a more immersive experience, but also giving the option to see everything for those who feel more confident in a lit environment.

The main key is not to overload the senses. On occasion, I've tried to add too many elements to a sensory space, which can be too much to process. I'm very much a fan of establishing each layer – whether that be a visual item or sound – letting it 'sit' for a while and allowing the audience to process what's happening in their own time and in their own way, with facilitation if required. Keep it simple; do it well.

FIGURE 2.1 Creative Director Claire Sundin using one of the many ways to explore a sensory glitter ball with her son, Charlie, in an Embracing Arts circus workshop.

Photograph by James Heatlie Photography

Corinna Laurie is the clinical lead occupational therapist at the **National Autistic Society** and author of *Sensory and Motor Strategies* (3rd edition, Jessica Kingsley Publishers). Here, Corinna shares her tips for creating sensory spaces.

Creating Sensory Spaces

Corinna Laurie

- When creating sensory spaces, it is important to know your audience. Work together with the person and be mindful of sensory differences.
- The carpet texture and fabrics on chairs, cushions and beanbags should be considered.
- Ensure there are ways for the lighting and sound to be altered. Offer eye masks, caps and coloured lens glasses to alter the light. Have ways to block the noise or add calming background noise/white noise.
- Add a sensory bag to the area with a range of supports for the pupil to choose to aid regulation (eg, ear defenders/noise-cancelling devices, fidget toys, visually relaxing toys such as oil jars and chewable objects/crunchy snacks).
- Use weighted blankets, lap-pads and hug cushions.

Lynne Castle, a qualified higher-level teaching assistant with over 25 years' experience, fosters a passion for helping learners at **St Giles' School** explore and access the world in a sensory, meaningful way. Lynne, who has had the privilege of leading her own classes, creates engaging and inclusive learning experiences for all. Here she shares her top tips.

Creating Sensory Spaces: Access to the World in any Space

Lynne Castle

- **Keep a 'box of tricks' ready:** A mobile box, trolly or bag filled with versatile items is invaluable for creating a sensory space on the go. Simple tools such as scarves, ribbons, small lights, mirrors and textured objects can transform any space into an engaging environment within minutes. Having this toolkit ensures you are always ready to create something special for your learners.
- **Experiment with mobile lighting:** USB-powered lights are a fantastic addition to any sensory space. They don't require PAT testing, as you can use a mobile USB phone charger. They are portable, giving you the flexibility to create and explore in any space. I have used different lights, allowing the learner to experiment with colours and effects. Use with reflective surfaces or translucent materials to create dynamic and mood-enhancing visuals. Lighting is an easy yet transformative way to create a calming, exciting or exploratory sensory atmosphere.
- **Use large pegs for instant transformations:** The large pegs typically used to secure towels on holiday can double as a game-changer for sensory spaces. Use them to secure shower curtains, large wallpaper sheets or pieces of fabric over doorways, furniture or walls. Some large pegs are fluorescent and then become a part of the learning environment. My favourite is a plain white curtain – perfect for projecting visuals or creating shadow play. These lightweight, portable setups can turn any area into a magical, immersive world.
- **Encourage flexibility and personalisation:** Find out what the learner enjoys, is interested in, likes and dislikes. Speak to the parents – this is a good starting place. Sensory spaces should evolve with the learner. Build in opportunities for choice using different access methods depending on the learner's needs and allow time for responses. Record their vocalisation and use this to create a personalised environment.
- **Engage all the senses:** Adding textures, sounds, smells and offering gentle massage movements to the learner within your spaces can transform the experience and boost focus and attention. I love the sounds and smells of popping candy – just putting a small amount in a paper cup or tin with a little water produces a wonderful sound perfect for connecting themes, stories and topics. I have used this on many occasions for rain, fireworks, autumn leaves crunching or the crackle of a warm fire (campfire); this can also be a calming auditory input, creating a soothing effect. The different flavours and scents of popping candy can allow the learners to engage in their senses, promoting curiosity and discovery.

Dr Julie Calveley is a learning disability nurse and founder of **NAC Wellbeing**, a community interest company dedicated to the emotional wellbeing and mental health of children and adults with severe and profound intellectual disabilities. Here, Julie shares her tips for creating meaningful and enjoyable sensory experiences supporting emotional connection and wellbeing.

Top Tips for Creating Meaningful and Enjoyable Sensory Experiences for Individuals with Profound Intellectual Disabilities, Supporting Emotional Connection and Wellbeing

Dr Julie Calveley

- **Prioritise attunement:** Tune into the person's feelings and needs to foster a sense of safety and connection.
- **Allow time:** Be patient. Processing sensory experiences often takes longer than expected. Embrace pauses and give time for responses.
- **Be responsive:** Observe and interpret all forms of non-verbal communication – what you see, hear and sense. Respond sensitively to these cues.
- **Focus on detail:** Experience the space from the person's perspective. Adjust anything that seems unsettling or ineffective.
- **Embrace repetition:** Repeated exposure builds comfort and predictability, helping the individual communicate preferences and gain a sense of control.

The next part of the book explores many different sensory spaces – some 'off the shelf' and ready to go, others requiring a little creativity and imagination. It is written as an A-Z with case studies, ideas in action and photographs, enabling you to see the concepts in practice.

Part 3

AN A-Z OF SENSORY SPACES TO SUIT ALL BUDGETS

DOI: 10.4324/9781003601364-3

A Activity Arches

An activity arch is a play structure designed to support hanging toys and other sensory-stimulating items, promoting cognitive and motor sensory development. Arches can be attached to wheelchairs or used freestanding on floors with the sensory space user lying underneath. They are portable and easily disassembled for travel or storage. Arches provide a blank canvas for creating fun and stimulating activities.

Using an Activity Arch

- Lay a comfortable blanket or mat on the floor and place the frame on a flat surface.
- Offer the sensory space user the option to choose their favourite sensory items from a selection. These can include interactive toys, lights, musical instruments and tactile, scented and textured items.
- Arrange the items and fasten them to the arch to encourage interaction through reaching, kicking, grasping and pulling.
- Invite the sensory space user to lie underneath the arch, positioned so they can see and reach the hanging items.
- Gently guide their feet, hands or elbows to the items, then explore together.
- Regularly change the items to keep the activity exciting and interesting.
- Supervise play.

For older children and teenagers, theme the arch with memorabilia related to their favourite football team, music band or hobby. Other ideas include theming by sound or light; attaching exercise cards; or using the arch as a hanger for a smartphone or tablet.

Emma Murphy, known as 'Little Mama Murphy', is a special needs teacher and mum to Hugh and his older brother Sean. Hugh has a rare chromosome disorder. Hugh is entirely unique – at present, there is no one else in the world with his exact rearrangement of chromosomes. Hugh was gifted an activity arch. Here, Emma shares her ideas on accessorising arches.

Hugh's Activity Arch

Emma Murphy

I decorate Hugh's arch to match the seasons or special events such as Christmas, attaching a variety of tactile objects Hugh can play with independently: coloured scarves, sound makers and other objects that will encourage him to reach and grab.

I made a Halloween-themed arch using items I either had in the house or bought from the pound shop, including an orange balloon I drew a face on, a dangly spider and a shoving set. Hugh loves fiddly, wiry objects, so these were perfect and fitted in with the Halloween colours.

FIGURE A.1 Hugh interacting with his Christmas-themed activity arch.
Photograph by Emma Murphy

B Beach Shelters

Beach shelters and windbreaks are easily adapted to create fun and cosy sensory spaces. Their pop-up design enables quick assembly and disassembly. They are available in various sizes, colours and designs, with different features such as UV protection – ideal for outdoor use on hot days.

Tips

- Secure an outdoor beach shelter with sandbags or stakes to stop it catching in the wind.
- Choose a beach shelter with good ventilation to keep the sensory space user(s) cool and comfortable.
- Place the shelter directly on the ground or dig a trenchlike space in the sand and place the shelter over the top to create a cave.

Katie Prestage is the founder of **Sensory Soup,** a melting pot of specialist sensory resources for those who teach, support and care for children and young people with complex learning difficulties and disabilities. Katie created an 'Under the Stars' sensory beach tent – the perfect space for storytelling or imaginative play, or for learners to relax and listen to the sounds of the night and the crackling campfire.

Under the Stars Sensory Beach Shelter

Katie Prestage

The idea came from working in an SEN school, where I was responsible for the sensory room. I always wanted the sessions I shared with learners to be magical. You can create magical experiences in a sensory room, as you can make it dark. As a child (and adult), I always loved the magic of camping – sitting around a fire under the night sky – so I wanted to recreate this experience for our pupils, many of whom had never had the opportunity to go camping.

I shared the session during the summer term as part of a 'Holidays and Outdoor Adventure' theme. Using a beach shelter, I created an 'Under the Stars' tent, adding sleeping bags, pillows, fake grass and a pretend fire from an ocean wave sensory light set to yellow, alongside natural sticks and neon tinsel.

Projecting twinkling stars onto the wall enhanced the magical environment and created a visual window for learners to stargaze in the night sky.

The Under the Stars beach tent offers many interactive learning opportunities. Learners can gather around a 'campfire' and experience the warmth of a wheat bag, the popping of bubble wrap, crunching paper that recreates the sounds of fire and the scent of freshly popped party poppers to evoke the smoky aroma of a real campfire. Use sticks and marshmallows to pretend to roast treats and sing campfire songs, creating an immersive and engaging experience.

Once the campfire fun winds down, investigate the night-time excitement further by turning off the fire and switching on torches, ready to listen to the sounds of different nocturnal animals and explore sensory boxes related to their characteristics and habitat. For an owl, feathers, bark and the scent of pine; for a fox, a faux-fur scarf for its tail, a backscratcher for its claws and the smell of fresh earth; for a mouse, a wind-up mouse nestled in a bed of leaves, fibreoptic wands representing the whiskers that it uses to navigate around its dark environment and the scent of apple.

Outcomes

The learners whom I shared this experience with loved it. It was fantastic to see how they explored and played independently, alongside me or with their class friends, using their imagination: building a fire with sticks and tinsel; pretending to warm their hands and roast marshmallows; putting the fire out and using their torch to explore in the dark; climbing into their sleeping bag and pretending to go to sleep in the tent.

FIGURE B.1 Under the Stars beach shelter.
Photograph by Katie Prestage

(Please note that the imitation campfire is inside the tent for photographic purposes)

You can recreate a camp indoors or outdoors using a bivvy, canvas, camouflage-patterned material, mosquito net, parachute, scrim net, tent or sleeping bag. Bring grasses, pinecones and leaves from outdoors to create an authentic experience. Provide binoculars and a camera, and introduce roleplay, providing camping clothes and cooking utensils. Learn about camping etiquette and fire safety; share a story or enjoy music.

B Balloon Arches

Balloon arches can be purchased readymade or are easy to make using balloons and balloon tape, which has holes for placing the ends of the balloon through to create a straight line. Attach the balloons to a rail, sticky-back wall hooks or a retractable washing line.

Experiment using different colours, shapes, sizes and colours of balloons; embellish using silk flowers, ribbons or streamers. Double link the balloon arches to accommodate multiple users and aid wheelchair access.

Julie Cowpe-Stephens and Helen Dillon are the founders of **Simply Sensory Training & Support Ltd**. They have many years' experience and expertise working with children and young adults with complex learning, sensory and physical disabilities, within both SEN and mainstream settings. Julie and Helen, together with Jacob and his mum Hannah, created an arch using balloons.

UV Balloon Arch and 'Jacob Fest'

Julie Cowpe-Stephens and Helen Dillon, with Jacob and Hannah

What a wonderful experience for the sensory explorer to sit under this balloon arch among the ribbons and look up at their UV balloon canopy! Place a fan on a light setting to gently blow the balloons and ribbons to make them move.

We made a rainbow arch using fluorescent paints, materials and balloons, giving the rainbow a new element of UV visual enhancement.

We added another sensory exploration element by placing items that smell inside the balloons (eg, Coco Pops); you can theme the smells.

FIGURE B.2 UV rainbow balloon arch.
Photograph by Simply Sensory Training & Support Ltd

'Jacob Fest' came about because this term, we explored and experienced all things festivals – from spring/summer to colours, flowers and music festivals. Shae Cheetham (Jacob's other home tutor) and I (Julie) made the rainbow spinner (see page 104) for the colour festival.

Following on from the colour festival, we explored music festivals. Hannah used the rainbow from the spinner and added it to the arch along with balloons and other fluorescent resources that Jacob painted as part of his learning and exploration.

We had such fun getting messy with shaving foam that was added to paint to give it a nice texture. We poured fluorescent paint into empty bottles and gave them a good shake and roll.

We made necklaces using dry pasta mixed with fluorescent paint and flowers using polystyrene balls that Jacob rolled in the paint and balloons.

At the end of the music festival, Jacob and his family celebrated Glastonbury in their garden using the resources we made with him. They had such fun! All the family love getting involved in Jacob's sessions. Jacob is an amazing young person and a true pleasure to work with. He really does give his sessions his all.

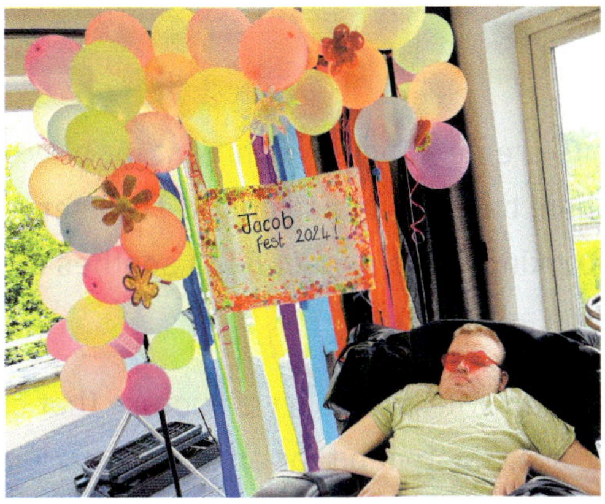

FIGURE B.3 Getting ready for 'Jacob Fest'.
Photograph by Simply Sensory Training & Support Ltd

Jacob very sadly passed away in March 2025, before this book was published. His memory is cherished by all those who had the privilege of knowing him and his legacy continues to shine in the hearts he touched.

B Ball Pits

The colourful balls in ball pits create a fun environment for play, helping individuals improve their motor skills, coordination, balance and strength. They serve as a therapeutic space as the sensory feedback from sinking into a pool of balls soothes and stimulates the senses, aiding regulation and reducing anxiety.

Remove the balls and you are left with a sensory structure that can be adapted for indoor or outdoor use. Drape fabric over the ball pit for an instant dark den. Promote sensory integration skills, helping people process information by replacing the balls with other stimuli (eg, feathers, leaves, pinecones or foam).

Teachers from the High Support (HSP) Curriculum Team at **Cerebral Palsy Alliance Singapore School (CPASS)** created a sensory space combining a ball pit and sensory umbrellas.

Ball Pit

CPASS

Aligned with our curriculum theme, 'Our School', a sensory space featuring a variety of sensory umbrellas and a ball pit were thoughtfully designed to engage and stimulate students' senses in an interactive and enjoyable manner. This space also serves as a platform for fostering understanding and connection, allowing teachers and peers to learn about one another's preferences (eg, likes and dislikes) through the exploration of the unique elements on each sensory umbrella. The experience was extended into the classroom, where students created their own personalised sensory umbrellas, incorporating items that reflected their individual preferences and interests.

FIGURE B.4 Ball Pit.
Photograph by CPASS HSP Curriculum Team

B Baths and Hydrotherapy Pools

A sensory bathtime provides an enriching and enjoyable experience, offering developmental, emotional and physical benefits; sensory stimulation through multisensory engagement; and reduced anxiety and stress through the warmth and buoyancy of the water and scents. It enables people to react to and communicate their sensory preferences; enhances mood and feelings of wellbeing; and, through the routine of bathtime, provides predictability and security.

Learning experiences can be supported in baths and hydrotherapy pools. Explore colours and objects, floating and sinking, and cause and effect; watch water beads expand, bubbles pop and bath bombs dissolve. Use gentle water jets to build muscle strength; enjoy a floating storytime using props.

Sensory Bathtime Activities

- Provide interactive toys, plastic bottles and objects that squirt water when squeezed, squishy balls and water wheels.
- Explore different water temperatures.
- Explore textured items, floating objects (eg, boats), swimming toy animals (fish, turtles, rubber ducks), rough and soft sponges, brushes, loofahs, mitts and washcloths.
- Incorporate music and sound to change the atmosphere using waterproof speakers.
- Promote cognitive skills using foam letters and numbers which stick to the bathroom tiles when wet, bath crayons and paints.
- Use bath bombs, bubbles, oils and water beads to change the colour, smell and texture of the water and add visual interest.

Lucy Williams is a proud mum to Thomas, a happy little man who happens to have profound and multiple learning difficulties (PMLD). Thomas has polymicrogyria, microcephaly and cytomegalovirus (CMV). Here, Lucy shares her top tips for creating additional sensory experiences in the home environment.

Bathtime

Lucy Williams

Thomas loves his bath and has a bath spa mat which produces a jacuzzi-like effect.

We use a variety of products for Thomas to have different sensory experiences in the bath on different days, including scented soaps, shower gels and soaps of different textures (eg, foaming soap and slime soap).

Previously, when Thomas was having a bath in the dark, we added lighting effects. We used bath lights in the past, but without much success, so we bought battery-powered light strings and put them in jars where we can secure the lid (eg, large Nutella jars).

Thomas now has a new projector to enjoy watching while bathing.

FIGURE B.5 Thomas enjoying a sensory bath.
Photograph by Lucy Williams

Emma Pauley is an artist, designer, researcher, public speaker, campaigner and award-winning entrepreneur who, through her business, **People as Partners**, is dedicated to ensuring that disabled people and carers are supported to live a good life. Emma's youngest daughter, **Millie**, was born with a very rare genetic condition called TUBA1a. Shaving foam wash is a huge hit in Millie's house, as Emma explains.

Sensory Bathtime

Emma Pauley

Bathtime is a very sensory part of the day for Millie and she loves foam to be squeezed under the water because it makes a huge squelching noise! Millie squishes the foam on the cold tiles and rubs it in.

I sing songs to Millie, such as: 'Wash, wash, wash your hair; wash it until it's clean. Big splash, big splash; now it's nice and clean.'

The reason I sing songs is the association of Millie's anticipation with what will happen next (ie, a song with the related activity). We sing 'Shake, rattle and roll' for getting dried.

B Beaded Door Curtains

Beaded door curtains reduce light and noise and act as a barrier against draughts. They are lightweight and easy to install, and are available in a variety of sensory materials – such as wooden or acrylic beads, bamboo, fabric, faux crystals, fibreoptic lights, metal, plastic, string (macramé), tinsel or decorated with seashells or feathers – making them perfect for creating sensory environments or a visually stimulating private separate space within a room that provides tactile and auditory feedback as the curtain strands click together and swish when moved.

(As with all structures, supervise at all times.)

Sophie Davey, SEN early years lead at **Manor Green Primary School**, West Sussex, created a roleplay shower corner for their 'All About Me' topic to explore hygiene and handwashing. The effect of the water from the shower was made using bubble wrap and ribbons; and an iridescent textured bathmat was placed on the shower base and accessorised with water sprays for the children to wash their hands, with sponges for texture exploration.

FIGURE B.6 Shower corner.
Photograph by Sophie Davey

B Bedrooms

Create an inviting, calm bedroom space that provides a soothing and engaging environment by incorporating sensory elements such as adjustable lighting, blackout curtains/blinds, soft textiles, scents and favourite personal items.

Emma Murphy, known as 'Little Mama Murphy', is a special needs teacher and mum to Hugh and his older brother Sean. Hugh has a rare chromosome disorder. At present, there is no one else in the world with his exact rearrangement of chromosomes – Hugh is entirely unique. Here, Emma shares ideas of how to create a sensory space in a bedroom.

Making Sensory Elements of a Bedroom Accessible

Emma Murphy

I bought blackout blinds and curtains for Hugh's bedroom so that his whole bedroom can be a sensory room. He has starlight projectors that can project onto the ceiling or onto a pull-down screen at the end of his bed.

Using the ceiling track hoist is a great way to create a sensory space in his room. I've hung a parachute from it, draping it over his bed so he's enclosed in a little tent, and then used battery-operated disco lights so he's enclosed in a riot of colour. At other times, I'll hang things for him to reach for and bat at – parrot toys are great for this, as they often make sounds as well.

UV lights make a dark space so much more interesting. I use UV strip lights and torches to illuminate individual items. We used fluorescent crayons to draw patterns on the bumpers inside his bed and shone UV light on them. Sometimes, we paint our faces and bodies with fluorescent face paints. I found a pair of pink gloves that glow beautifully under UV light and Hugh and I can spend ages touching our glowing pink hands together. I think Hugh's favourite is a cheap piece of pink washing line that he tangles in his fingers – it looks incredibly bright under the ultraviolet torch.

To make the sensory elements of his bedroom accessible for Hugh, he has recordable switches that say, 'Alexa, turn on the bubble tube' or 'Alexa, turn on the starlight.' It's a simple piece of technology but it allows Hugh to have control over his space.

B Bed Canopies

Bed canopies are open structures which can be enclosed by draping material over the top, attached to a wall or placed over a person lying in a sleeping bag or on a beanbag, cushions or a mat on the floor.

Use as a den or hang sensory items from the canopy arms for exploration.

If using outdoors, the poles can be pushed into the ground to provide instant shelter from the sun.

FIGURE B.7 A bed canopy used as an outdoor sensory space.
Photograph by Sarah Hall

B Bedsheets

Sheets can be draped over existing furniture or features to create a sensory space. Explore different colours and textures; and enhance the sensory experience by spritzing a little scent or a couple of drops of essential oil onto the material.

Emma Pauley is an artist, designer, researcher, public speaker, campaigner and award-winning entrepreneur who, through her business, **People as Partners**, is dedicated to ensuring that disabled people and carers are supported to live a good life. Emma's youngest daughter, **Millie**, was born with a very rare genetic condition called TUBA1a. Millie is a big sensory seeker and together they consider sensory experiences in all that they do.

Making the Bed

Emma Pauley

When making the bed we use the duvet as a big parachute. Millie squeals with excitement from the anticipation of this activity. She loves it! Millie lies flat on the bed under the covers; I count to three, then lift the duvet up fast and high and let it fall back down on top of her. I count to three and repeat the process. This is a great activity for morning and bedtime, or when you are changing the bed linen. It provides proprioceptive feedback (it's also a workout for the carer's biceps too!).

Dr Joanna Grace is a sensory engagement and inclusion specialist, researcher, author, trainer, TEDx speaker and founder of **The Sensory Projects**. In all of her work Joanna seeks to contribute to a future in which people are understood despite their differences. Here, Joanna talks us through how to create a shadow theatre.

Shadow Theatre

Dr Joanna Grace

You will need:

- an overhead projector or light;

- a bed sheet or a white shower curtain;
- cardboard;
- Sellotape; and
- sticks.

Instructions

- Hang a bedsheet or a white shower curtain to create a screen.
- Use an old overhead projector to project a light onto the screen.
- Stand someone between the light and the screen – they see a high contrast image that moves when they move, so it is responsive. Responsivity of environment is critical to early communication, for so many reasons!
- Add cardboard ears to that person or Sellotape on a different nose. Now you have a character on the screen and as you move, you act as you play the role of someone else.
- Create a shadow puppet to hold on sticks between the light and the screen. The puppet and the person can interact. By moving closer to or further from the light, you cast a bigger or smaller shadow – great for performances of *Alice in Wonderland*.
- Cut out a little paper shadow and lie it on the projection plate. These paper shadows can interact with people and puppet shadows. For an example, see the rainbow fish paper shadows created by a class of early years children in Figure B.9. It doesn't matter how good your scissor skills are – any shape can count as a fish; and with a hole punch and a little coloured cellophane, each one has a shiny scale.

FIGURE B.8 The Angel.
Photograph by Dr Joanna Grace

FIGURE B.9 Rainbow fish made by a class of early years children.
Photograph by Dr Joanna Grace

For shy actors or nervous people, performing behind the screen is perfect – you can't see the audience, but you can see and monitor your own performance.

You can create moving scenery, special effects and much more ... I used to run entire weeks of teaching on this; left to my own devices, I'd have merrily taught the whole curriculum through shadow theatre! You just need paper and a light. It's wonderful; and its simplicity –even in an age of special effects – has an atavistic, awe-inspiring property that all hearts bend to.

B Blankets and Throws

A blanket or throw has many uses. It can provide comfort and enhance social interaction through a 'blanket hug', or serve as a base for a sensory activity for those who prefer floorwork. Blankets make excellent backdrops for storytelling and imaginative play: a ruffled-up blue blanket with water spritzed on it becomes the waves of the sea; or a silky blanket becomes a sheet of ice, with the effect made more authentic if it is placed in the freezer before the activity. Invite the story explorer to place a blanket over their head to simulate a train entering a dark tunnel, re-enact hiding in cave or enjoy a magic carpet ride.

Match themed blankets (eg, stars or animals) to fit your story. Swish the blanket to recreate actions such as flying or wear it as a superhero cape for adventures.

Create a cosy den by draping a blanket over furniture or a retreat using different textured blankets.

FIGURE B.10 A patchwork blanket used to deliver an Elmer sensory story. Photograph by Jane Mullen Speech Therapy Ltd

Secret Safe Spaces

Chris Barson, founder of Positive About Autism

If you ever enjoyed hiding away under the bed as a child, you will be in touch with the solitude afforded by a secret and safe space. This is a need in autism and other neurodivergent ways of being. Children on the spectrum need a place to 'recuperate' from the social – somewhere that has nothing to do with people or language and interaction. Secret safe spaces afford a child the opportunity to calm the brain, assimilate experiences and learning, and fortify themselves for more.

B Body

'We are all rich sensory environments. Even in an empty space, you can offer multiple sensory experiences through moving, sound, touch and even through your choice of perfume or clothing,' write **Jane McLean** and **Ruth Spencer**, dance artists who have developed **Cheshire Dance's 'Wanna Dance?'** Artist in Residence in Adult Social Care Programme. 'Wanna Dance?' – a collaboration between **Vivo Care Choices** and Cheshire Dance – is about co-creating one-to-one dancing opportunities with people with profound intellectual and multiple disabilities. The programme asks whether participants would like to dance and, if so, what that dance might look like. Here, Jane and Ruth share their guidance.

Our Bodies as a Sensory Environment

Jane McLean and Ruth Spencer

You are Enough

Tap into yourself as a sensory being. What do you notice about your own sensory environment? What can you see? What can you hear? What do you notice inside your own body? Commit to spending time 'being with' your partner. Minimise distractions. Notice the sensory experiences that emerge when you are together: the blink of an eye, the squeeze of a hand, the sound of a breath.

Consent is Key

Stay open and aware of how you are feeling while noticing what your partner is communicating about how they are feeling. How does your partner communicate 'yes' and 'no', what they like and don't like? Meet them in the moment; give space for what emerges. It might be different from what you imagined. Dances can be big, small, gentle, vigorous and everything in between.

Touch is a Sensory Environment

When used sensitively, with care and ongoing consent, touch offers a unique non-verbal sensory environment and point of connection. Hand-to-hand touch is often a good place to begin. As you and your partner come into contact, feel the texture, temperature and shape of their hand. Touch is a two-way experience.

Take a moment to consider how their hand is touching you. We can 'listen' through touch to the small dances: fingertips curling, uncurling, relaxing, sliding, squeezing. Move with your partner: allow them to take the lead and follow what is there.

Be Curious

Be open to the dance that is emerging between you and your partner. Questions encourage curiosity. Ask yourself: 'What is moving? How might I respond to that movement? How does that movement/stillness feel? How is my partner responding? What am I learning through moving with my partner?'

Follow your partner's interests. Through our dances, we have discovered different people's movement preferences – for example, small, patient hand dances; large, galloping, travelling dances; and dances of push and pull. We have also learned what additionally supports these dances, such as favourite soundtracks, lots of space, exploring reflections in mirrors/windows and creating our own sounds with voice and instruments.

Keep Learning

Capture and reflect upon what happens. In 'Wanna Dance?', we record what happened: movements we noticed, what worked well/what didn't work so well and what we saw in our partner to confirm this. We regularly review our learning with support staff, families and households.

FIGURE B.11 Hand to hand: Adam Sass and Jane McLean.
Photograph by Abbiegale Blake

References

Grace, Joanna (2018) Sensory-Being for Sensory Beings. Routledge.

C Canvas and Tarpaulins

Canvas is a natural fabric made from cotton or linen with a textured, woven surface. It is a versatile material for sensory activities due to its durability, breathability and resistance to tearing. Its absorbency makes it an ideal base for collaborative art projects. Enhance storytelling by painting scenes and characters onto the canvas or use it as the base for a sensory wall, a surface for building blocks or small world play.

Made from PE or PVC with a smooth, plastic-like texture, a tarpaulin is a cheaper option. It is fully waterproof, providing strong weather protection, and is thus ideal for outdoor use. Attach to a fence using rope, bungee cords or zip ties to create a temporary shelter; or attach to poles inserted into the ground, adjusting the height to make a crawling space. Use dark colours to create a dark space or a transparent tarpaulin to maximise light. Lay on the ground for a waterproof sitting area; add sand for an instant sandpit; or use indoors as a base for messy play.

C Cardboard Boxes

Lightweight and versatile, cardboard boxes are ideal for constructing temporary dens, play or sensory spaces that can be easily dismantled and recycled when no longer needed. Cardboard boxes can be cut, taped, drawn on and decorated – skills requiring hand-eye coordination, dexterity and precision. Alternatively, place assorted-shaped boxes to build a den (igloo style), engaging planning and problem-solving skills to ensure that the structure is stable; or fold the ends open to create tunnels when attached together.

Motivate children to eat more fruit by building a cardboard box fruit stall, standing the box upright and cutting out a serving hatch.

Transform into boats, rockets and spaceships for roleplay. Cut slits in the boxes to create turrets and build a castle.

Create a homely effect by glueing wallpaper cutoffs and textured objects (bubble wrap, felt, foam, sandpaper) to the inside to make tactile walls. Paint, draw on and decorate the outside. Retailers such as Hobbycraft sell easy-assemble, ready-to-decorate cardboard playhouses, shops, trains and castles.

Cardboard boxes can be sourced from grocery stores, electrical stores and motorbike dealerships. Ask the office staff in your setting to keep the boxes they receive deliveries in.

Friends **Aayesha** and **Liberty** got creative at a **MakerWorld** craft event organised by **The Children's Art School**. Funded by The National Lottery Community Fund, the Children's Art School offers free, artist-led experiences for children aged two to 16 and their families. At this event, MakerWorld attendees created 3D representations of existing and imaginary Dewsbury places.

Dewsbury Town Hall

Aayesha and Liberty

We used pictures from around Dewsbury town to make Dewsbury Town Hall. We used cardboard boxes, a black marker, paints, pens and double-sided sticky tape. We had such a great time using the boxes and choosing the paints and using them with brushes and our hands to create colours and patterns to bring the building to life. We worked as a team to paint and create, and from design to finish, we had fun experimenting and trying new ideas. We really enjoyed painting the building and we can't wait to see it at the exhibition.

FIGURE C.1 Dewsbury Town Hall, by Aayesha and Liberty.
Photograph by Rebekah Clee

Sarah Hall, the founder of **Willows Sensory Service**, is passionate about sensory ideas and approaches and enjoys sharing ideas. Sarah works from her sensory room at her home in Shirley, where she delivers bespoke sessions for individuals based on their needs and interests.

Sarah made a *Frozen*-themed castle in her sensory room with her son and nephew. The castle was decorated using spray paint, bubble wrap and iridescent cloth with purple and blue shimmering shades. A light-up bathmat was placed inside to add an element of enchantment. The snow effect was created using a homemade effect wheel. Sarah pierced a circle of paper with a needle and placed it in a blank effect wheel holder.

FIGURE C.2 *Frozen*-themed castle.
Photograph by Sarah Hall

Sophie Davey, SEN early years lead at **Manor Green Primary School**, West Sussex, made a glowing cardboard gingerbread house using screen dividers as extra support. Battery lights were placed into laminating sheets stapled into cylinders, with the sealed battery packs hanging out then wrapped in cellophane. The cylinders were stapled to the house. The inside of the gingerbread house was decorated with candy canes made by painting cardboard tubes with red and white stripes.

Cardboard structures make an excellent base for themed activities. Place props inside a cardboard castle to promote roleplay. Provide materials for making swords and shields, dressing-up clothes and costume jewellery.

Incorporate sensory activity ideas into your structure. Here are some ideas based on a cardboard gingerbread house:

- **Arts and crafts:** Make gingerbread men using brown paint and a pastry/Playdoh® cutter. Add ginger powder or grated ginger to the paint for an extra sensory element.
- **Design and technology (D&T):** Make craft stick gingerbread man puppets or salt dough decorations.
- **D&T food:** Make gingerbread men biscuits or decorate shop-bought gingerbread men with icing and decorations. Offer a vegan/gluten-free option.
- **Literacy:** Promote listening, speaking, comprehension and sequencing skills by placing copies of *The Gingerbread Man* book in the house.
- **Sensory bin:** Create a river and sandbank by placing water, sand, grass, leaves and bark chippings on a large tray. For a less messy option, lay green or brown fabric or artificial grass on the floor as your base and use lentils or dried beans as your sand. Add scoops and containers to promote fine motor skills and small world play items to spark imagination.

- **Gingerbread mouldables:** Mix flour, oil and ginger powder or grated ginger root. Tailor the mixture: to create a firmer dough to build finger muscle strength, add more flour; or add more oil for a looser consistency.
- **Listening skills:** Play a listening game or sound bingo using audio clips linking to the story – for example, woodland sounds, a spoon mixing in a bowl, an oven door opening, a kitchen timer, running footsteps, animal sounds (a cat, dog, cockerel, pig, cow, fox) and a flowing river.
- **Sensory story:** Place a box of props inside the house for sensory space users to enjoy a sensory story. Suggested props could include the following:
    - Gingerbread man: Biscuit, foam or felt shape.
    - Oven: Heated wheat bag/handwarmer/hairdryer.
    - Lady: A handkerchief sprayed with perfume.
    - Man: Aftershave, fake beard.
    - Cat: A Slinky toy.
    - Dog: A squeaky dog toy.
    - Cockerel: Feathers.
    - Pig: A curly pink pipe cleaner.
    - Cow: A fake chamois leather.
    - Horse: Two plastic beakers/coconut shells.
    - Fox: A feather duster/wind-up teeth.
    - River: Place water, mud and leaves in a water bottle, seal the lid and shake.
- **Problem solving:** Set up a gingerbread man treasure hunt. Hang and hide cardboard cutouts or felt gingerbread men in the house for sensory space users to find. Provide clues. Explore prepositions.
- **Roleplay in a baker's shop:** Provide hats and aprons, utensils, gingerbread men, money, a cashbox or till, trays for displaying wares, and a phone and notepad for taking orders. If working in a group, allocate and encourage role swapping (baker, customer, sales assistant, biscuit/cake decorator, delivery driver). Provide arts and crafts materials to make badges.
- **STEM:** Build a strong and stable bridge for the gingerbread man to cross a river using sticks, glue, cardboard, string and other building materials.
- **Science:** Grow ginger from a root.

Sensory Boxes

Sensory boxes are versatile and are easily tailored to suit individual interests. Place sensory items in a shoebox to invite sensory exploration. Ideal for tabletop or lap tray explorations, they can contain a person's favourite items or be themed; or you can create an 'All About Me' sensory box.

FIGURE C.3 Autumn-themed sensory box.
Photograph by Victoria Navin

FIGURE C.4 Simplified sensory box. Swap items out if the person shows little interest or becomes bored of them.
Photograph by Victoria Navin

'All About Me' Sensory Box

This is a communication passport or profile in the form of a box filled with sensory items that represent an individual. They are a tool for people involved in someone's life (teaching teams/activity coordinators/support workers) to learn and understand about that person's life, likes and interests.

In a school setting, the boxes can be set up to welcome new students and are useful in the autumn term when students change classrooms, as they can explore their boxes with one another, fostering engagement and building friendships.

In an adult setting, the boxes can be used when a resident moves into a setting or new daycare provision.

- Offer a choice of boxes and the option to personalise through decoration.
- Together, explore sensory items that relate to the person's life, providing choices so they can explore and express their sensory preferences. If working in an educational setting, use the student's communication passport as a tool to help you.
- Involve family, friends and other people involved in their life.
- Regularly update the box, adding new items as the person encounters new experiences (eg, a seashell from a seaside trip).
- Include an item to represent an event in the future.

CASE STUDY: REUBEN'S ALL ABOUT ME SENSORY BOX

Reuben is 14 years old. He attends a special school.

I created categories (in bold type below) around the items Reuben selected; these can be tailored to suit the person.

- **Me:** Reuben's favourite activity is riding his adapted bike. We explored bike-related sensory items (a bicycle pump, a bell and a mirror). Reuben chose the shatterproof bike mirror. Reuben's bike mirror straps onto his wrist and is a hands-free option, helping promote self-awareness.
- **Born:** This could be an item relating to the person's identity. Reuben was born in Manchester and enjoys going to Manchester United's home football matches. We explored a football programme, keyring and scarf. Reuben liked the tactile feedback of the scarf.
- **Family:** Reuben chose his favourite photograph of his mum, dad and sister from a selection of three. Alternatively, the person could draw a picture of their family members or carer.
- **Dad:** Reuben's dad works away during the week. We explored a selection of his dad's socks and ties. Reuben choose a striped tie, which we spritzed with his dad's favourite aftershave.
- **Music:** Reuben enjoys wearing ankle bells when riding his bike, so we placed a set in his box along with a recording of him singing made using a sound button.
- **Relaxation:** Reuben finds relaxation through hand massage. We tested a range of scented and unscented creams. Reuben chose a strawberry hand cream.
- **Holiday:** Reuben went on holiday to Spain over the summer. His mum sent in a magnet embossed with a sunshine and palm trees, which Reuben likes to rub on his chin. I placed different denominations of euro coins in the box for Reuben to explore with the magnet.

- **Future event:** Reuben will be a pageboy at his brother's wedding in November and he will be wearing a bowtie. We placed this inside his box, as Reuben feels a little anxious as he has never been to a wedding before. Talking about this and wearing the bowtie are helping Reuben prepare for and look forward to the event.

Life Story and Memory Boxes

Sensory life story and memory boxes can also be used to help people process loss and grief through reflection, sharing memories with others and on anniversaries. Choose a box that feels special and select personal and cherished items that remind you of the person. You can add notes and a letter explaining the significance of the items for future generations.

Memory boxes can be made in preparation for a person's passing, as well as afterwards.

C Carpet Tiles

Carpet tiles are a cheap resource, available in many colours and textures. Your local carpet shop will often gift them. Use as a sensory pathway, a weighted lap mat or textured fidget tile, or a visual background (by placing white items on a black carpet tile). They can also be used for sitting inside sensory structures, as activity mats for defining individual sensory activities, to place small parts on or as a base to prevent sensory items from rolling away. They can be used to promote learning through colour sorting or be flipped to play a memory matching game.

I created a tactile corner in an EYFS classroom by gluing carpet tiles to two adjoining walls, extending from the floor upwards.

C Cavendish Spaces

Helen Edgar, the founder of **Autistic Realms**, and **Ryan Boren**, who helped to start **Stimpunks**, have been exploring Cavendish spaces, which are based on flexibility, interaction, movement and the role of embodied responsive experiences.

Cavendish Spaces

Helen Edgar and Ryan Boren

A Cavendish space provides a rich sensory experience that can enhance and expand learning experiences for those with PMLD.

Like Cavendish, Ryan and I are autistic, so we relate to much of his personal and professional life. Cavendish's cave was his personal sensory and social cocoon. His life, as well as Thornburg's concept of alternative learning spaces, has inspired our adoption of caves, campfires and watering holes as essential components of inclusive multisensory spaces. Here we share our ideas of how these can be created in your setting or at home.

Caves are spaces for quiet reflection and self-directed or interdependent exploration, recovery and rest.

Tents and gazebos are examples of on-the-floor cave spaces and can accommodate a person's physio equipment; side lyers, positioning wedges, cushions, beanbags, wheelchairs or standing frames. Incorporate lighting effects and have a basket of favourite items nearby; attach items using Velcro. Personalise by adding a scent a person likes so they can begin to associate it with their cave space, developing a feeling of safety and familiarity over time.

Campfires are spaces for learning with a storyteller, teacher or carer, offering time and space to explore different sensory experiences, next steps and a rich learning experience. Examples include messy play, sensory stories, story massage, themed sensory explorations (moon sand, shaving foam, bubbles), switch-activated toys and technology.

Watering holes are spaces for social learning with or alongside peers and carers – a wonderful opportunity for co-regulating, exploring and experiencing things together and joining in parallel play. This type of space allows connections to develop at a more profound emotional level and enables social skills and communication to evolve through participation in a small group. It develops trust and creates a shared meaning which can enhance trust and relationships.

Examples of watering hole activities include shared sensory messy play, shared trays or mats of paint to explore with different body parts, baskets or a hanging clothes rail with musical instruments or sensory toys for people to engage with/reach out for with their feet/hands/arms and shared immersive themed scenes (eg, woodland).

Setting up different activities people can access, experience and share together can be meaningful and bring joy. It is an opportunity to build relationships and form new connections, and can enhance some learning experiences. The activities can be easily adapted for different positions and people's care needs if you take time and plan things ahead. We can't force a sense of belonging, but we can create an environment to enable it to emerge.

References

Thornburg, D. (2013). From the Campfire to the Holodeck: Creating Engaging and Powerful 21st Century Learning Environments. John Wiley & Sons.

C Colour Wheels and Light Projectors

Often found in sensory rooms, colour wheel projectors are lightweight devices that cast lighting effects to stimulate the senses and promote calmness. The wheels are available in a range of colours and effects (liquid or print, bubbles, camouflage) and themes (the ocean, fire, galaxy, woodland, animals) that can be used in your topics/sensory stories.

FIGURE C.5 Heart wheel projected onto a tent.
Photograph by Sarah Hall

Sarah Hall, founder of Willows Sensory Service, projected a colour wheel onto an umbrella which was placed in a tent decorated with tinsel and lights. A peg spinner with shiny baubles was suspended from the umbrella's arms. A basket filled with festive scents – such as cinnamon, clove powder, citrus fruit, cranberry, gingerbread, peppermint and pine – was placed on the floor, covered with a net curtain and a sheepskin rug.

FIGURE C.6 Christmas tent.
Photograph by Sarah Hall

C Cupboards and Small Rooms

Cupboards or small rooms are often disorganised and filled with clutter. Sort through the clutter, box it up or move it elsewhere and you have a functional area you can transform and maximise space. As these areas are smaller, they can be a more affordable option than larger spaces and offer greater flexibility, as they can be easily adapted and changed or themed as needs evolve.

Ruth Poole, SENCO at **Ellel St John's Church of England Primary School** in Lancaster, and her team are very passionate about their sensory room, reporting that it has helped students to self-regulate and has had a positive impact on their engagement and behaviour in school.

Sensory Break Room

Ruth Poole

We put our sensory room in place after the Covid-19 pandemic to support the children's transition back into full-time education. Each class already had a calm corner; many were made around the book corner, but we noticed that students didn't get the privacy they needed, so we decided to make a special room.

Converted from a former art and D&T stock room, our sensory break room was designed on a budget of a few hundred pounds.

The hard flooring has been covered with carpet tiles left over from a class refurbishment. An LED light strip hangs on the wall, and a projector projects abstract images and rainforest sounds. We also have sensory circles and mats with liquid paint in them, a fish light tube and a gym ball. Pictures on the wall promote emotional regulation and deep breathing techniques.

The beanbag sofa was donated; large cushions and soft toys provide sensory feedback and comfort. We have a desk with activities: fidget toys and items to manipulate; poppits, magnets and a Tetris puzzle.

The biggest cost was the electrician's charge for installing plug sockets.

All students have access to the room. Some have a regular slot; those who don't can request one. Five-minute breaks (using a sand timer) are timetabled into the children's schedules and they can return later in the session if they wish.

It's good to see how many places now have sensory rooms – for example, football stadiums, airports and train stations (eg, Manchester Piccadilly's assisted travel lounge).

We are now looking for a second space, as the need is increasing. We are noticing that as the Covid-19 babies are now in education, some children are finding regulation of emotions difficult. They missed out on social interaction, as there were no parent and toddler groups during the pandemic; but then they started school and were suddenly plunged into a class of 30 other children.

The sensory break room has been such a positive introduction to our school. I can't recommend it highly enough: be bold and step out in support of the children's mental health needs. Our room measures 3.2m x 2.4m, so your space doesn't have to be large.

FIGURE C.7 Sensory break room.
Photograph by Ruth Poole

C Curtains

A curtain attached with rings to a curtain pole or with hooks to a rail, or threaded onto string, cord or a retractable washing line, creates an instant sensory space.

Use different fabrics to change the light – for example, chiffon, cotton, crepe, hessian, lace, muslin, net, and satin create an airy atmosphere; while heavier materials such as chenille, corduroy, denim, fake fur, suede, velvet and wool can be used for a darker ambience.

Explore various textures, including crocheted, glossy, knitted, metallic, quilted, ribbed, sequined, smooth and woven fabrics. Charity shops are a cost-effective source of curtains; they will often either offer curtains with small flaws (eg, a rip or mark) at a reduced price or donate them.

Add a few drops of essential oil or a spritz of spray/perfume onto the material to enhance the sensory experience.

A fun activity at the start of a new term or for an 'All About Me' topic is to set up a photobooth. This helps students to bond and captures moments in time. Repeat the activity at the end of the school year and compare the photos.

Choose an easily accessible area with space for exploring props and taking photos. Use a curtain or a choice of two curtains as a backdrop. Set up a box containing assorted hats, clothes, face paints, feather boas, gloves, masks and wigs for students to explore new looks. Attach props to wooden sticks: balloons, funny lips, beards and moustaches. Aid creativity by adding card signs and blank speech and thought bubbles for students to write in. Set up the camera and show participants how to use it, encouraging them to swap roles between taking photos and being photographed.

D Dens

There are many skills involved in den building. It affords opportunities to explore D&T through building and construction; experiment, make mistakes and problem solve in a safe environment; build physical development; foster cooperation, turn-taking and listening to others' ideas; and build communication skills through teamwork.

Dens can be built using everyday items and things found in nature, such as straw, hay, dried grasses and sticks. Work around existing features – play equipment, trees, a gazebo, a washing line – or, if you have willow, make a willow dome. Use brown tape, bulldog clips, clothes pegs or cable ties to secure your structures. Drape a sheet, blanket, piece of fabric/material or duvet over a desk or two chairs in an indoor setting, or underneath open stairs in a home setting.

Build Your Own Den Kits

There are many ready-to-built kits on the market with simple instructions. www.thedenkitco.com has themed dens – pirate, forest, cottage garden – and an Ed Stafford shelter. The kits comprise a groundsheet, tent pegs, rope and mallet, which come packed in a bag. They foster exploration and imagination in children regardless of age, enabling them to construct a shelter to shield themselves from the elements or engage in roleplay in the great outdoors or within the comfort of home.

You can also buy sets comprising sticks, balls and connectors that create a shell.

Corner Dens

By utilising a corner of an outdoor space where two fence panels or railings meet, you can make a sensory area using minimal materials with a pre-existing frame. Attach a tarpaulin, waterproof canvas or plastic sheeting to your structure, then pull out to create a sloping roof. Use a groundsheet to provide additional insulation and protection from moisture

Sophie Davey, SEN early years lead at **Manor Green Primary School**, has set up a Rainbow Corner sensory space in the outside area where two fences join. The theme of the space changes regularly to match topics they are currently exploring.

FIGURE D.1 Pirate den.
Photograph by Unstuck Studios

FIGURE D.2 The Rainbow Corner.
Photograph by Sophie Davey

Richard Hirstwood, the director of **Hirstwood Training Ltd**, works worldwide delivering training in the area of SEND to help improve the lives of children and adults. He is passionate about breaking down barriers to sensory learning. Here he shares his ideas on creating sensory corners.

Creating Sensory Corners in Classrooms and at Home: Why, What & How

Richard Hirstwood

Sensory corner spaces provide a structured environment in which learners can engage in multisensory exploration, learning activities, relaxation and self-regulation. The adaptability and simplicity of a sensory corner make it a workhorse in your sensory approach to learning.

What is a Sensory Corner?

Sensory corners are dedicated areas that allow learners to engage with sensory stimuli in a controlled and structured manner. These spaces can range from elaborate sensory set-ups in special education classrooms, with bubble tubes and fibreoptics, to smaller, more cost-effective sensory corners created using portable or everyday sensory materials.

In classrooms, sensory corners offer a flexible learning environment tailored to meet individual learners' needs. Teachers can adapt these spaces to suit curriculum topics, using sensory objects and tools corresponding to specific learning goals. At home, sensory corners provide a calming, engaging space for children to regulate their emotions and explore sensory materials in a more personalised environment.

Sensory corners are crucial in encouraging cognitive and physical development for learners with severe or complex learning needs. These learners often rely on tactile, visual and auditory stimuli to help them engage with the world around them. Sensory corners offer a safe, controlled environment in which they can experience a range of sensory inputs without becoming overwhelmed. For example, you can introduce tactile toys, lights and gentle sounds to support learners in processing sensory information at their own pace.

Learners with neurodiverse needs, particularly those with autism or attention deficit hyperactivity disorder (ADHD), also benefit from sensory corners. Sensory overload is a common challenge in busy, visually or auditorily stimulating environments. Sensory corners provide these learners with a retreat. In this space, they can self-regulate and take a break from the overwhelming demands of the classroom or home environment. With appropriate sensory stimuli, such as soft lighting, textured objects or calming sounds, learners can regain focus, making it easier to re-engage with learning activities or home routines.

Sensory umbrellas and pop-up tents offer a unique addition to sensory corners at home and in classrooms. These tools provide a more enclosed space within the corner, allowing for a deeper sense of focus and privacy. Sensory umbrellas with hanging objects or lights create a visually stimulating environment while reducing distractions from the surrounding space. They are particularly effective in helping learners with visual impairments or those who are sensitive to bright or fluctuating light.

Conclusion

Sensory corners, whether in classrooms or at home, are vital for supporting learners with PMLD and neurodiverse learners. They offer a flexible, personalised space in which learners can engage with sensory stimuli in a controlled manner, fostering cognitive development and emotional regulation. Tools such as sensory umbrellas and pop-up tents further enhance the sensory experience by creating a focused, private space within the corner. By offering learners a place to retreat, explore and self-regulate, sensory corners contribute to a more inclusive and supportive learning environment at school and home.

Indoor Den

A den can be a secret hideaway; a place for adventure, games or socialising; or a sanctuary for relaxation. Den building encourages physical activity, creativity and problem-solving skills, fostering cooperation, communication and collaboration. Blankets, sheets, duvets, sleeping bags, cushions, pillows, rugs and blankets are great materials to use.

Sarah Hall, founder of **Willows Sensory Service**, demonstrates the multiple benefits of children collaborating to make an indoor den.

The Indoor Den

Sarah Hall, with Chelsea Pettitt and Matt

My son Matt and his friend Chelsea built a den when they were children. He was very into building dens back then and was very inspired by all of Chelsea's equipment. He dragged it into the lounge. Chelsea directed from her wheelchair under the blue blanket and the two of them thought the whole thing was both fun and funny – their giggling was infectious.

They had to ask for help from adults with placing some of the sheets, but the decisions on where things should be placed were definitely down to the two children.

The skills they demonstrated building their den included teamwork – they worked well as a pair, bouncing ideas off each other. At the time, Chelsea's speech was not always clear, so alongside communication skills, she was persistent and Matt was patient. They both demonstrated initiating ideas and problem solving. To cover Chelsea, they needed something higher than the wheelchair, so they used the mobile hoist.

At the time, it seemed like they were just playing together; but looking back, Matt would have been following instructions, furthering interaction skills and developing the confidence to share his ideas too.

Once the den was built, they shared the space together, chatting, eating snacks and giggling in their own self-made little secret world.

FIGURE D.3 Chelsea and Matt inside their den.
Photograph by Sarah Hall

Sarah showed me video footage of the day her son Matt built a den at home with his friend Chelsea. It opens with Mathew arranging his football duvet cover over a chair to create a doorway. 'That's my door,' he says.

'What would you like to say about the den?' Sarah asks him. 'It's fantabulous!' he replies. 'Every den needs a door.'

The camera pans to Chelsea, who is sitting beaming in the den. A white blanket is tickling her head as she moves. 'We've just put the blanket here and then we made a doorway,' she giggles.

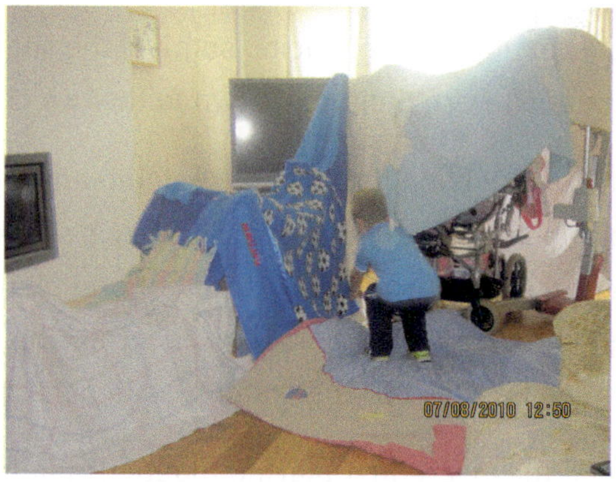

FIGURE D.4 Matt making the doorway to the den with Chelsea under the blue blanket.
Photograph by Sarah Hall

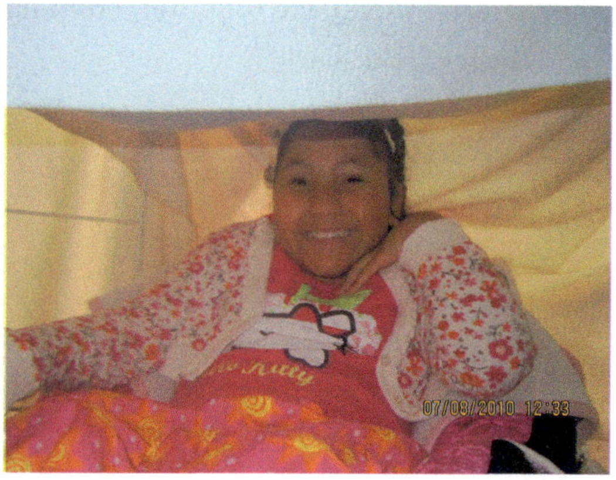

FIGURE D.5 Chelsea sitting under the tent.
Photograph by Sarah Hall

Sarah turns to other people in the group who are enjoying watching the den building. 'This is an amazing den-making experience – I've never seen anything like it in my life,' says Adult A.

'This is just fantastic – you must be the best den builders in the entire universe,' smiles Adult B.

The footage cuts to the end of the den-building experience and we hear music playing. Chelsea is sitting in the den singing along to '(Is This the Way to) Amarillo' by Tony Christie.

I spoke to Chelsea, who is now an adult, while researching this book. She recalls: 'I was feeling excited because I had never made a den before and it was a good experience for me.'

D Dröna Boxes

Dröna boxes are folding fabric storage containers designed to fit IKEA's Kallax shelving units. Available in a range of colours and textures, they are excellent for storing and organising resources, can double up as a sensory bin for housing light resources and can be used in creative play.

To support our Alice in Wonderland theme, we used Dröna boxes to set the stage for students to perform magic shows. We made wands and magician's hats using craft paper and cardboard tubes, and wore bow ties, capes, waistcoats and gloves. Our box of magic props included a deck of cards, coins, cups and balls, dice, handkerchiefs, a magic trick set, soft toy rabbits, sock puppets and rabbit ears. We used bells, chimes, cymbal crashes and drumrolls, and made fanfares using kazoos to create magical sound effects, punctuated with silence to draw the audience in.

The activity promoted confidence, creativity, planning, fine motor coordination, patience and perseverance, as the students practised their tricks.

Gwyn McCormack, a qualified teacher of vision impairments and director of **Positive Eye**, delivers courses and creates unique programmes – including Positive Looking and Marvin's Story Time Show – to support children, families and schools in meeting the needs of children with vision impairment and complex needs. Gwyn shares how to use a Dröna box and an ability communication board to house a high-contrast resource.

FIGURE D.6 LED light box made using battery lights placed inside a Dröna box. Photograph by Victoria Navin

Dröna Boxes and Ability Communication Boards

Gwyn McCormack

The background is what the child looks at when they look at you or at the resource. Create a backdrop to house a high-contrast resource to maximise the opportunity for visually directed reaching. The Dröna box is cheap and folds away for neat storage. Other suggestions include painting a cardboard box black; pegging a piece of black cloth against a tent wall; draping a black sheet over a screen and pegging in place; or using a black A2 communication board which opens out to three panels to create a space for placing resources and/or attaching items/symbols on the nylon-coated lip fabric using hook dots.

Keep the environment you are showing the resources in decluttered: show one or two objects to begin with and build on this. Create a collection of high-contrast resources or collect high-contrast resources of different sizes and colours to explore.

Vision is the major way a child understands the world – it plays a greater role than all the other senses in accessing the environment. Keep vision at the forefront of your mind when creating a sensory space.

FIGURE D.7 A Dröna box housing a high-contrast resource.
Photograph by Gwyn McCormack

FIGURE D.8 A black communication board on a black tabletop.
Photograph by Gwyn McCormack

E Eco-nooks

Embrace outdoor learning, promote biodiversity and support your local ecosystem by leaving a wild area for native plants to grow and wildlife to thrive. Simple steps to take to support an eco-nook include hanging bird feeders; providing a water source (eg, a pond or birdbath) or solar fountain; scattering wildflower seeds; making a dead wood and leaf litter pile to create habitats for insects, fungi and small animals; attaching nesting boxes to trees; composting; and harvesting rainwater. Building a small hide near your eco-nook provides a base to enjoy activities such as creating 3D artwork using nature items, enjoying a picnic, exploring a nature sensory bag, making bark and leaf rubbings and observing nature.

The students at **Hillside Specialist School and College** use half-tents as a hideout from which to watch nature and spot birds, as SEN teacher **Christy Townson** explains.

Half-Tent Hides

Christy Townson

Julie Greenall (forest school leader) set up the tents in our forest school garden area.

My class used the half-tent hides last summer term to watch wildlife and birds from. Classes made bird feeders with Julie and we spotted many birds in the garden, including robins, chaffinches and goldfinches.

Our school is surrounded by fields and we have lots of trees on the grounds, so we get lots of squirrels, rabbits and minibeasts to spot. Julie made a bug hotel out of wood with the older students in our college. We saw bees nesting there last summer. We have reared butterflies from caterpillars and this is a great place to spot the butterflies from when they are released.

The hides also provide students with a different environment to sit, learn or stim in when outside.

One student in my class, who can be unregulated in the classroom environment, is a different girl when at forest school and particularly enjoys standing under the tent and swaying, getting relief from the sunshine and watching the sun patterns and light cascading through the tent. This student learns better when outdoors, so I incorporate maths and word learning into the outdoor environment.

Weather permitting, we use the school grounds and the forest school garden as much as we can. We have tuff trays, a polytunnel nearby for our gardening, a vegetable patch, a mud kitchen and a forest area.

Being outdoors enables the students to explore on their own terms and promotes movement, which in turn helps sensory regulation. Once in a place ready to learn, the students can begin to concentrate on the tasks in hand with more motivation, given the sensory and natural elements to a lot of our learning when outside.

We have painted and created artworks outside, some under the half-tent, looking at what we can see in the garden or using the paints and colours as a sensory experience, to communicate emotions or just to have fun with the materials.

One child in my class had had a regression in communication and had become very frustrated and self-injurious; but being in the forest school garden, spending time under the half-tents and playing with water had a positive effect on his mental health and he began to use his picture exchange communication system (PECS) again when in this area. He was soon able to request 'forest school' when becoming unregulated and was able to walk and spend time there to become calm, before reaching crisis.

All my students find communication and word learning more motivating when asking for things outside. We use PECS, theme boards and Makaton signs when in these areas. I have made 'nature finders' by cutting a square in an A4 sheet in the middle and laminating it and adding known PECS to the children around the outside. The children had to (physically) zoom in on an object, such as a flower, almost 'capturing' it in the finder; then they could tell an adult, using the words/visuals around it, what they had found.

FIGURE E.1 Nature and bird-spotting hide.
Photograph by Christy Townson

Tips for Setting up a Wildlife Hide

- Choose a safe, quiet location with good visibility of the surrounding area where wildlife passes. Utilise woodland, trees or the bottom of your outdoor area.
- Scrim net, camouflage material and netting blend the hide into the surrounding environment, minimising disturbance and increasing the chance of birds and wildlife coming closer to the hide. Involve sensory space users in collecting grasses, leaves and twigs to further conceal the hide.
- Hanging bird feeders and having a birdbath nearby will help to attract birds.
- Be as quiet as possible and explain that sensory space users should not touch or approach any wildlife, as they should not be disturbed in their natural habitat.
- Take a drink, a healthy snack and a first aid kit.
- Dress for the weather.
- Provide binoculars, a wildlife guidebook, worksheets, camera and a notebook to record observations. A tripod or mount for the binoculars and camera aids steady viewing.
- Create an interactive experience by enjoying a scavenger hunt, wildlife bingo or nature arts and crafts.

Indoor Nature Space

Bring the outdoors inside by incorporating elements of nature into your sensory space: floral patterns, earth tones and natural materials such as wood and natural fabrics. Set up a sensory box and place natural items in a basket (eg, plants, grasses, pinecones, leaves, feathers). Theme by month or season.

F Fishing Nets

Fishing nets are lightweight, with a flexible fine synthetic mesh. Secure to a wall or corner space or suspend from the ceiling to hang and display sensory items. For a beach-themed sensory net, tuck and tie barnacles, cuttlebone, driftwood, kelp, a mermaid's purse, seaweed, shells, starfish and seagull feathers onto the net. Record the sound of crashing waves or seagulls onto a sound button. Spritz the net with coastal room spray.

Incorporate the net into a sensory story, draping it over the story explorer to recreate being caught like a fish or captured by pirates. Add props to the net as the story unfolds to create a visual narrative; or make a treasure hunt net activity by placing objects in the net for students to work together to retrieve (eg, compass, coins, eyepatch, Jolly Roger flag, old maps, toy jewels, toy cutlass, sandpaper shapes and seashells).

G Gardens

Outdoor areas will differ depending on your location and the space available. Some of you may have raised beds for growing flowers, fruits, herbs and vegetables; others a sensory garden.

If space is limited, garden in containers (eg, recycled tyres make cheap planters and can be painted); use tiered planters; wall mount waterproof shoe storage hangers containing plants inside the pockets; use handled felt bags for portability; or explore vertical gardening (see 'Trellises' on page 152).

Plastic water bottles can be effectively repurposed as terrariums, offering an innovative and sustainable solution for creating miniature ecosystems.

Plastic Bottle Terrarium

- Cut off the top quarter of the bottle and set aside.
- Use the bottom three-quarters of the bottle as your terrarium.
- Add soil to the base of the bottle, plant your seeds or plants and water them.
- Place the top quarter of the bottle back onto the base as a lid by gently squeezing it to fit.
- The bottle top can be closed to maintain warmth or removed to allow air circulation.

Upscale using larger water bottles.

Carol Allen is an education adviser for information and communications technology and inclusion and a Bett Awards judge, and has been a panel member and contributor to sessions at the House of Lords for the All-Party Parliamentary Group for Assistive Technology Committee.

Carol remains at heart a teacher who is a passionate advocate for inclusive practice that follows Universal Design for Learning principles. Each child can connect, communicate and be taught by using a sensory approach to the educational environment.

Over the past three years, Carol has been involved in creating a sensory garden in Cumbria, based at The Estate in Patterdale, which is owned and operated by YMCA North Tyneside. Carol explains how the garden was created as an area for contemplation and sensory exploration and outlines the many benefits of sensory gardens.

The Sensory Garden

Carol Allen

A long, long time ago – in the days before the National Curriculum, which promised a blueprint for education but conveniently ignored the educational needs of a huge section of the student population, in particular those working primarily at a sensory level – we were free to create experiences and activities that matched the needs and interests of our students. Yes, I am that old!

If it snowed, we could stop what we were doing and go outside and 'play'. We could take the minibus to beaches and forests without acres of planning and follow what is now called a 'child-led' learning pedagogy. We could take children who had barely left their immediate home area on trains to London – even on day return flights to Ireland – with relative ease.

Work early in my career demonstrated clearly that sensory activities in the outside environment – whether a garden, forest, beach, shopping centre, cinema or plane – had a much greater impact than those replicated in a classroom environment. Touching snow while outside breathing the frosty air; feeling the tingling on your cheeks and the swirling of the air; hearing the sounds of crunching underfoot – these were immersive experiences, rather than simply hands placed in a tray of snow in the warmth of the classroom, with the smells of the dining hall and the sound of music from the next classroom intruding on the experience. The sensory focus was more defined, more holistic and therefore more authentic.

Over the past three years, I have been involved in creating a sensory garden in Cumbria, based at The Estate in Patterdale, owned and operated by YMCA North Tyneside. An undeveloped area opposite the office, right at the entrance to the estate, was kindly offered for this mini-project. The aim was to create an area for contemplation and sensory exploration. The location meant that it could be seen and experienced by both visitors to the estate and the many passersby who ventured through the gates to explore the area and walk to the lakeshore.

In keeping with the values of the YMCA, one objective was to keep the area as environmentally natural as possible, in addition to using recycled materials and repurposing items that were no longer useful. So, we explored the darkest corners of the shrubs, bushes and overgrown areas, locating old and broken chimneypots, buckets, wheelbarrows and wooden structures.

Two old benches were revived and placed so people could rest and enjoy the peace. Local slate and woodchip were used for simple paths with a few reclaimed paving slabs near the main bench. Plants were chosen to 'work', such as blueberries to feed the birds and squirrels, and a simple herb garden of lemon balm, rosemary and thyme, offering smells as well as textures to explore. A wheelbarrow became a mint garden (check out how many different varieties of mint we can choose from!), so that smelling and touching could be strengthened by picking the leaves and mixing them with hot water to make mint tea (with attention to safety). A mirror was strategically placed deep in the background to provide light reflections. A solar fountain was added to a plant-pot water feature to add sound and movement to the space. One tree was planted which will create dappled light through its leaf structure as it grows. We found a broken stand for hanging baskets under a long discarded pile of 'bits'; now restored, we have a combination of hanging baskets and bird feeders, which are emptied daily.

Most excitingly, we put up feeders to support the local population of endangered red squirrels, who moved in very quickly and can be seen every day – usually in the morning and evening.

Sensory learning in our garden engages the senses – sight, sound, touch, taste and smell – in a natural environment. This approach helps all individuals connect with the natural world while also enhancing their cognitive and emotional development. The garden was designed for everyone; we are ALL sensory learners and benefit from time experiencing the world we live in. So, what does this offer to anyone who stops to look, sit or interact?

Multi-Sensory Engagement

The garden naturally provides stimuli that can engage all five senses, such as the following:

- **Sight:** Observing the colours, shapes and movements of plants, animals or landscapes.
- **Sound:** Listening to the rustling of leaves, birdsong or flowing water.
- **Touch:** Feeling the texture of tree bark, leaves or rocks.
- **Taste:** Sampling wild foods (with safety and proper knowledge).
- **Smell:** Smelling flowers, soil or rain.

Enhanced Cognitive Development

Engaging with nature through sensory experiences promotes cognitive skills such as observation, memory and problem-solving. It encourages curiosity and helps children (and adults) develop critical thinking through direct, hands-on interaction with the environment.

Physical and Emotional Benefits

The combination of sensory experiences in nature can lead to increased relaxation, reduced stress and enhanced mood. Physical activities – such as hiking, walking and even touching nature – can boost physical health and improve mental wellbeing.

Mindfulness and Connection to Nature

Sensory learning outdoors promotes mindfulness, encouraging individuals to be present in the moment and connect with the environment. This fosters a deeper appreciation and respect for nature.

Exploration and Discovery

Sensory learning encourages exploration, where individuals can freely discover and make sense of the natural world. They might notice subtle changes in the environment or come across new elements they might not typically encounter indoors.

Enhanced Creativity

Nature is often unpredictable and dynamic, which can spark creativity. Children and adults alike can use their sensory experiences as inspiration for artistic endeavours, such as drawing, writing or storytelling.

Development of Environmental Awareness

Sensory learning fosters an awareness of natural patterns, ecosystems and biodiversity. It can help individuals better understand environmental issues and encourage a sense of stewardship towards the Earth.

Personal Growth and Self-Confidence

Navigating natural environments and experiencing sensory learning can help individuals build self-confidence. Outdoor learning often involves challenges and problem-solving, enhancing independence and resilience. We plan to introduce simple tasks and activities which can be used if desired.

Social Interaction

In outdoor sensory experiences, group activities (eg, nature walks, games or tasks) can foster social skills and cooperation. These encourage sharing experiences, talking about observations and working together in a collective setting.

Conclusion

By combining the sensory experiences of the natural world, sensory learning can be a holistic, enriching and engaging way to learn and grow – whether for children, adults or communities. We still have plans for the next stages of the garden but are finding that a gradual approach is proving less intrusive for the natural world we are adding to and reshaping.

Why not try something yourself? Remember, it can be simple: even bird feeders or a mint garden will offer so many activities. Enjoy!

FIGURE G.1 The sensory garden at The Estate, Patterdale. Photograph by Carol Allen

FIGURE G.2 A red squirrel spotted in the sensory garden. Photograph by Cat Morton

Allotments are another engaging way to connect people to the outdoor environment. They can be divided into areas for growing produce and creating sensory areas.

Ralph Booker – former autism training director at **Hampshire Autistic Society** (1996-2008), where he worked with Ron 'Nobby' Clark, head of day services – tells us more.

The Sensory Allotments and Stokes Bay

Ralph Booker

The Adult Development Service (ADS) was located in the grounds of an old manor house with a generous garden and a thick, wooded copse. The grounds backed onto Stokes Bay, a natural beauty spot and beach.

Primarily, the ADS provided daytime services and support for adults both from our residential services and from outreach sources – autistic young adults who lived with their parents or with other residential providers.

The ADS included a sensory room and outdoor sensory facilities which exploited the spacious grounds. There was also a sensory-based music room inside the ADS building.

Sensory Allotments

The ADS users worked with staff to create sensory-specific allotments. There were three-metre square parcels of land which included dry leaves, wood chips, a herb garden and soil. Some users liked to sprinkle themselves with these materials. The goal was to encourage sympathetic engagement. One user eased his severe anxieties by accessing the outdoor sensory facilities.

There were enough trees – coniferous and deciduous – to create a simple maze. Some users helped to gather fallen leaves that were bagged and dried in storage over the winter to be used again as dry leaves the next summer.

Goals

The goal of most sensory interaction was to create a new, more predictable world where social awkwardness was not a disability and where raw sensations could bring pleasure. Many ADS users asked for 'time out' in the sensory facilities.

G Garden Arches

Garden arches can be used to create a sensory space both outdoors and indoors. They are available in metal and natural materials such as willow and bamboo. Their design makes them easy to accessorise: lights can be threaded through them; lanterns and other sensory items can be hung from the wood and metalwork; fabric can be draped over the top; and spaces can be brought to life by adding speakers, sound buttons or items that make a noise when touched.

Sophie Davey, the SEN early years lead at **Manor Green Primary School** in West Sussex, is passionate about creating sensory spaces for learners and upcycled a garden arch for an interactive Avatar theme.

Avatar Glowing Arch and Ceiling Leaf

Sophie Davey

The frame for this sensory space is a garden arch secured to the floor using heavy boxes filled with sand. Flower-shaped fibreoptic fairy lights are entwined around the arch to create an interactive experience. If I were to update the arch, I would add bird sound buttons, toy bugs and smells.

Above the arch, fixed to the ceiling, is an IKEA leaf canopy to represent the glowing tropical land. The leaf canopy was upcycled by adding streamers and UV materials.

The IKEA leaf canopy creates a cheap, versatile mobile sensory space. Made of polyester, it is lightweight, so it can be easily fixed to a wall or ceiling or partially folded to create a cosy nook on the floor. It can be upcycled for many other projects. You can also recreate a leaf canopy by deconstructing an old tent.

FIGURE G.3 Avatar glowing arch and leaves.
Photograph by Sophie Davey

G Gazebos

Often used for extra space at fairs and sports days, or as additional learning spaces, gazebos are freestanding structures with a roof. Due to their size and open design, they are brighter and airier than tents, offering greater versatility in terms of use and placement. Their open sides make them wheelchair-user friendly and able to accommodate multiple people. Outdoors, they provide shade and shelter and can be used as a space for socialising, relaxing or taking part in activities. Where there is sufficient room, they can also be placed indoors and themed for immersive learning.

Aromatherapist **Bridget Robinson-Clark** uses aromatherapy to enhance the lives of people with life-limiting disabilities. Bridget has successfully run her business, **See Change**, for 20 years, offering massage and other related treatments to people.

Bridget's Hippy Tent is a great example of how you can adapt a gazebo combining strips of material and fabric with sensory items to create a multisensory environment.

Hippy Tent

Bridget Robinson-Clark

The Hippy Tent came about during the pandemic, when I was working full time as a support worker at a Wilf Ward Trust House. During this time, service users could not get out and take part in their usual activities, so the aim of the tent was to create a standalone stimulating environment and a sensory space to enjoy fun activities.

The fabric was donated through the power of Facebook. I cut the fabric using pinking shears, then sewed it onto tape, creating different layers. I added various fabric textures – the brighter the better – and attached pompoms and little bells for sounds and texture. I added drops of essential oils to some of the fabrics, so the space became as stimulating to as many senses as possible. We used our Hippy Tent for storytelling.

During the summer months, we attached the tent to a gazebo outside and enjoyed storytelling, picnics and craft activities in it. Many people just appreciated the feeling of the tent and the different textures it provided.

There are now plans to make the tent a permanent fixture in a sensory room. Once it is back inside, the plan is to add fibreoptic lighting to include further sensory elements.

I think the main benefits of the tent are due to how it is constructed and the fact that it's a stimulating, multisensory space for people who enjoy exploring different textures and colours.

FIGURE H.1 Hippy Tent.
Photograph by Bridget Robinson-Clark

H Hammocks

Hammocks create soothing and comfortable environments that aid regulation of the sensory system due to their calming, gentle and rhythmic rocking motion. Swinging provides vestibular input, promoting balance and coordination. The structure and fabric give deep pressure feedback, helping to decrease anxiety and aid relaxation.

There are different sizes of hammocks – single, double, queen and family – designed to be affixed to structures (trees, poles, posts) using straps or hooks, suspended off the ground or hung on a stand. Hammocks are available in a variety of materials; fabric hammocks comprised of durable materials can be used indoors or outdoors (some have built-in mosquito nets), and can be accessorised with blankets, pillows or cushions.

Jennifer Abbanat lives in Davis, California, USA, and is a parent to three neurodiverse children. Founder and owner of the company **Crow's Nest Advocacy & Consulting**, Jennifer shares how sensory swings have been a therapeutic tool to support her autistic child and her whole family.

Why a Sensory Swing?

Jennifer Abbanat

A sensory swing helps stimulate different parts of the brain that support a child's nervous system to regulate, be soothed, develop greater capacity, learn and engage in life. The act of swinging – whether side to side, back and forth or both – provides repetition, rhythmicity and improved spatial awareness, balance and motor coordination. It also helps reduce anxiety, promotes relaxation and therefore enhances wellbeing.

Depending on the individual, a sensory hammock swing can be used to calm down and soothe a hyper-aroused (dysregulated) nervous system; or it can also have the opposite effect on individuals who need more stimulation to 'wake up' a hypo-aroused (low-energy, under-stimulated) nervous system.

In particular, sensory hammock swings stimulate two main sensory senses in the body. The first is called the vestibular system. This system helps us sense gravity and orient ourselves in space – for example, detecting the directionality of what's up and what's down and helping orient our eyes and head in relation to our body. This sensory input helps to calm the body and supports balance, helps to regulate motor function and stimulates muscles and nerves to work in a more coordinated way. This all provides a heightened sense of security for the individual, which helps promote development and continued growth.

The second sensory system that is stimulated by swinging in a sensory hammock is the proprioceptive system. This occurs through using a Lycra-type fabric that provides a deep pressure, all-over 'body hug'. This input also supports sensory regulation of the nervous system, which can help calm an overwhelmed individual – not through cognitive processes, but through a body-up approach that uses the senses to reduce chaos and overwhelm and provide soothing effects, especially during a meltdown.

This is especially useful for many neurodivergent individuals who experience the world differently due to their more sensitised nervous systems, which often creates learning and thinking differences in a world that is not 'set up' to meet their unique needs. The proprioceptive system is governed by particular sensory receptors located in muscles, joints and tendons, and helps detect and inform the brain of joint position, movement and load. It is considered the body awareness system. The sensory receptors share information about where our body parts are without having to look at them, as well as how much force to use when holding an object (eg, a plum versus a hammer), pushing an object, throwing a ball and other coordinated movements, such as riding a bike.

These systems work together to enable an individual to move about and interact within their environment in a coordinated and confident way which is more organised and fluid and takes less cognitive effort, thus reducing stresses on the body. Sensory swings are a way to assist individuals with their focus, to support their learning and engagement. By reducing anxiety, they can help support social interactions that may at times be difficult for many neurodivergent children and adults.

Sensory swings can help individuals learn to better navigate their environments, with increased feelings of safety and ease. Dr Luke Beardon – autism advocate, senior lecturer in autism, author, co-editor and researcher – is famous for his quote: 'Autism + Environment = Outcomes.'

By supporting the individual through appropriate resources and a toolbox that matches their needs, a sensory swing can help them better navigate environments that can often lead to overwhelm, which can create chaos for many neurodivergent individuals. We can improve many aspects of an individual's quality of life, opening up opportunities for greater capacity, more joy, homeostasis and growth – which all humans deserve. These are outcomes we all need to achieve for our overall wellbeing. The most important feature of the hammock swing is that it is fun and a playful way to engage with a child. Research shows that if something isn't fun, there is no learning. This goes for both children and adults. So, get a hammock swing and experience the benefits for yourself and your family.

FIGURE H.2 Hammock suspended over a sandbox in the back garden.
Photograph by Jennifer Abbanat

Activity Hammock

A Lycra hammock sensory swing suspended over activities (eg, LEGO®, DUPLO®, jigsaws, puzzles, wooden blocks) helps provide deep, calming pressure through both vestibular and proprioceptive sensory input.

The set space of the hammock provides a low-distraction environment in which the person can focus on their activity, helping to improve cognitive skills and attention span.

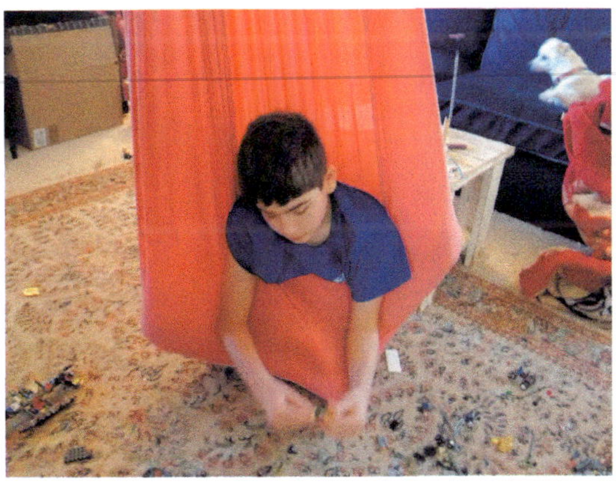

FIGURE H.3 Jennifer's son plays with LEGO while suspended from his hammock.
Photograph by Jennifer Abbanat

H Hoists

Hoists are devices to help lift and move individuals who need assistance with their mobility. They can be accessorised to provide visual stimulation from items that gently swing, vibrating items (eg, wiggle balls) and interactive elements such as light and sound.

When using a hoist as housing for sensory items, be health and safety aware. Do not place any heavy items on the hoist, remove items before using and supervise the activities.

Lucy Williams is a proud mum to Thomas, a happy little man who happens to have PMLD. Thomas has polymicrogyria, microcephaly and CMV. Lucy uses a hoist for visual/auditory feedback.

Thomas' Sensory Hoist

Lucy Williams

Thomas loves his bedspace. We utilise the hoist to hang things from for visual and/or auditory feedback, then position it above Thomas. For visual feedback, we use lights, tinsel and baubles, either together or separately. For auditory feedback, we use bells, windchimes and a hanging rainmaker, which make a noise if Thomas knocks them.

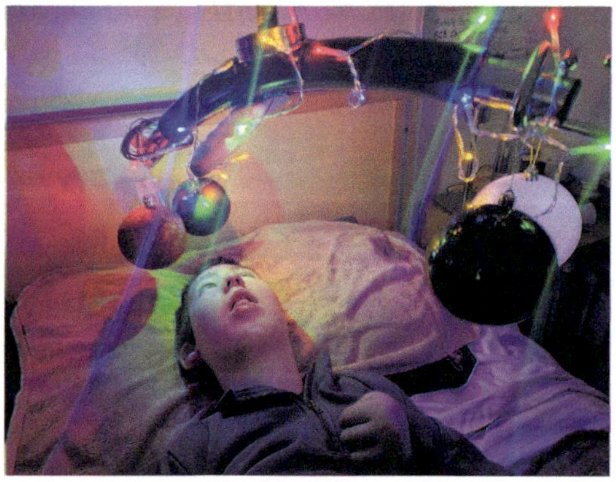

FIGURE H.4 Thomas exploring his sensory hoist.
Photograph by Lucy Williams

R Hula Hoops

A hula hoop is compact, portable and lightweight, making it suitable for suspending from the ceiling, using as a light feature or displaying items. It can be used as a mobile for hanging bells and sound-producing items or for forming sensory garlands by weaving in leaves, flowers and other natural elements. Drape fabric over the hoop to convert it into an enclosed space or attach a curtain to the hoop using curtain hooks. Tie strips of material, foil and beads to make a sensory curtain. Attach a shower curtain to the hula hoop using C-type shower hooks.

Ghostbusters Shower Hula Hoop

Sarah Hall, founder of Willows Sensory Service

I have a Ghostbusters shower curtain that I hook onto a hula hoop using shower hooks and play the Ghostbusters theme tune inside it.

Sophie Davey, SEN early years lead at **Manor Green Primary School**, West Sussex, used a hula hoop to create a Peter Pan/Tinkerbell experience for her students.

Peter Pan/Lost Boys/Tinkerbell Hula Hoop

Sophie Davey

This was part of our school production – our topic for the PMLD class I was working with was Peter Pan. We want to create immersive spaces without boundaries for learners with visual impairments and cerebral visual impairments, and a transparent but immersive hoop experience allows you to be in the hoop together.

How we use the hoop is responsive to the children's needs. This is where intensive interaction and a relational approach are so important, because we don't want to put children in situations which, bearing in mind their visual impairment or sensory need, become overwhelming. Each child is interacted with differently, so we adopt an approach of, 'Let's create this space together.' It could be on the floor; we could get inside the space and experience it; we could hold it upright so it is flat in front of the child, to provide opportunities for the initiation of the tactile response, and then move it around.

We do a lot of work on framing faces for children who are learning about 'What does this mean?' on another person. Doing this on a bigger scale creates a sense of immersion and allows you to bring a couple of children into the experience at the same time; whereas many of the other activities may be done in smaller spaces, using props such as hats, sunglasses etc.

We also use a hula hoop in the early years department, suspending it above the mark-making table and hanging pre-writing cards and letters from it, so that the children can imitate shapes and look up at it.

We wrapped ribbon around the hoop to change its colour, threaded green fairy lights around the ribbon and then hung crepe paper strips and streamers from the hoop.

FIGURE H.5 Peter Pan/Lost Boys/Tinkerbell hula hoop.
Photograph by Sophie Davey

Another idea is to create a sensory story hula hoop, hanging story props from the hoop so the children can become authors of their own stories.

I Intergenerational Sensory Spaces

Adults benefit from sensory spaces as much as children and teenagers do. For dementia patients, a calming environment aids relaxation, reduces anxiety and enhances overall wellbeing.

Intergenerational sensory spaces bring people of different ages together to share activities and are often found in care homes and community centres. Providing spaces and activities enhances social interaction between generations, leading to improved mental health, cognition and physical activity. Both sides benefit from connection: younger people can learn from the older generation, who in turn can share their knowledge and experience and gain a sense of purpose.

Tracey Allen runs a small company called **Made for Little Feet** and specialises in creating sensory stories for babies and toddlers.

Tracey ran a 'Snowy Day' baby and toddler session in a care home. Umbrellas were decorated with lights, tinsel and pinecones to make them sparkle. The residents enjoyed the sensory experience of being under the umbrellas too.

FIGURE I.1 Snowy Day sensory umbrella.
Photograph by Tracey Allen

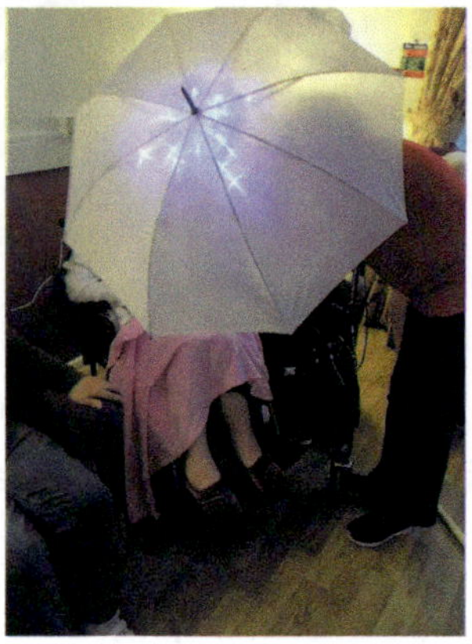

FIGURE I.2 A resident enjoying the Snowy Day sensory umbrella. Photograph by Tracey Allen

J Journey Sensory Pathway

A journey sensory pathway is a trail that engages the senses through auditory, olfactory, tactile and visual elements, promoting sensory exploration and development. Pathways can be created indoors or outdoors using a variety of materials, including bamboo, bubble wrap, clay, confetti, cork, cotton wool, decking, fabric, feathers, felt, foam, foil, grass/turf, hessian, jelly, leaves, mud, netting, pebbles, pompoms, plastic and rubber mats, sand, sandpaper, sponge and wool.

Tree stump hopping or following footprints spaced out from tiny steps to wide strides promotes gross motor skills and balance. Water paths incorporating different temperatures of water and portable solar fountains add interest.

Accessorise by placing bamboo chimes, bird feeders, bunting, dreamcatchers, fairy lights, feather garlands, hanging mobiles and ornaments, herb bundles, suncatchers, wind chimes and spinners along your pathway.

For indoor pathways, explore bubble paths using bubble machines, colour paths using carpet tiles, musical stepping stones or wind pathways using pinwheels and fans. Create a sensory pathway along a wall using scented and textured items or a glow-in-the-dark pathway using paints, UV items and UV torches to light the way.

Theme a pathway (eg, an easter egg hunt) or enjoy a story path bringing a book to life using elements from the story – for example, for the book *We're Going on a Bear Hunt* by Michael Rosen, incorporate grass, water, mud, forest leaves, a fake snow snowstorm and a blanket for story explorers to crawl under, representing a cave.

K Kitchens

Cooking and baking are sensory-rich activities. Consider the feedback from baking a cake, from the initial mixing of ingredients to the first delicious bite. The gritty sound as the sugar crystals crunch and scrape against the bowl, mixing with the smoothness of the creamy butter. The contrast in colour as the golden egg yolks land on the white, pillowy mound of sifted flour that falls like fine snow. The sweet, comforting smell of vanilla essence. The rhythmic sound of the whisk against the bowl and the slight resistance as you mix the ingredients into a thick batter that falls like molten silk when poured into the cake tin. The hum of the oven and the rush of heat carrying the sweet aroma of the baked cake in the air as you open the oven door. The crosshatch pattern of the metal cooling rack on which you place the cake. The slight bounce of the cake when you press it gently with your fingers. The feedback from squeezing icing though the nozzle of an icing bag; the sweet, sticky gloss of a glacé cherry on the top.

In addition, food preparation promotes cognitive and motor skill development as cooks use tools, fosters creativity, encourages healthy eating habits and builds independence.

Simple ideas include the following:

- **Baking:** Mix ingredients to make batter for biscuits, brownies and cakes; choose decorations.
- **Bread-making:** Knead and shape the dough; watch the bread brown and rise as it bakes.
- **Fruit:** Select, wash, peel and cut fruit to make fruit kebabs, a fruit salad or smoothie.
- **Muffin-mixing:** Provide a variety of mix-ins, such as blueberries, chocolate chips or bananas. Participants can mix the batter and add their chosen ingredients.
- **Pasta:** Explore the shapes of the different pastas; add ingredients to make pasta salads.
- **Pizza-making:** Make dough or use ready-made bases; offer a choice of toppings.
- **Sandwiches:** Choose and prepare ingredients to make a variety of fillings for sandwiches, paninis and toasties.
- **Vegetables:** Select, wash, peel and cut vegetables; make salads, soup, vegetable kebabs, stuffed vegetables and wedges.

Emma Pauley is an artist, designer, researcher, public speaker, campaigner and award-winning entrepreneur who, through her business, **People as Partners**, is dedicated to ensuring disabled people and carers are supported to live a good life. Emma's youngest daughter Millie was born with a very rare genetic condition called TUBA1a. Here Emma shares her ideas for weaving sensory experiences into daily routines.

Incorporating Sensory Activities into the Everyday

Emma Pauley

We love a good pot of soup in our house and Millie loves to help! I often make the soup at the table so she can join in. I fill a cold pot of water and put a range of vegetables in this, chopping them beside my child. Some vegetables, such as leeks, float; others, such as carrots, sink. Millie loves to mix the vegetables and explore their smells and textures. She is particularly fascinated with lentils and leeks and loves tearing leeks into small pieces. Millie also likes to explore the many different sensory layers of a pumpkin –the smooth yet firm outer skin; the cool, slimy pulp inside; the slippiness of the seeds; and the stringy, fibrous flesh which squelches as you scrape it out.

FIGURE K.1 Millie exploring a pumpkin.
Photograph by Emma Pauley

L Light Rooms

A light room is a specially designed space housing lighting and equipment to create a soothing atmosphere. These can include adjustable lighting, light panels and interactive displays reactive to touch or movement, UV lighting, LED curtain lights, bubble tubes, fibreoptic lights, image/patten projectors, interactive floor mats with lights and infinity mirrors.

The equipment can be used to create immersive learning environments by adding accessories and props. Here are some examples based on a space theme:

- fibreoptic light strands (starlight);
- floating light-up orbs (UFOs);
- glow-in-the-dark paint (nebulas);
- glow-in-the-dark stickers (stars);
- hanging planet mobiles (the solar system);
- lava lamp (alien slime);
- LED light strips (space craft);
- star projector (the Milky Way);
- UV figures of astronauts and aliens; and
- UV or light-up sensory balls (planets).

Chris Peak, managing director of **The Apogee Project** – a high-tech sensory and learning space supporting individuals with complex additional needs – believes that sensory light rooms are an invaluable tool for teaching foundational play and ICT skills to individuals with complex disabilities and brain injuries. Here, Chris shares his top tips for using sensory light rooms.

Sensory Light Rooms

Chris Peak

- Create a safe, engaging and adaptable environment in which learning, communication and play come together.
- Design your sensory room and activities to develop essential visual, motor and cognitive skills while addressing each person's sensory integration needs.

- Allow participants to explore and engage at their own pace and empower individuals to interact actively with their surroundings by incorporating technologies such as switches and eye gaze access.
- The design of a sensory room is critical to its success. Flexibility ensures that the environment is effective for a spectrum of sensory presentations. Some individuals benefit from calming experiences; others require stimulating input.
- Sensory rooms also excel at promoting communication. Integrating tools such as communication boards and speech-generating devices enables individuals to express preferences and share experiences.

M Mosquito Nets and Insect Screens

Mosquito nets and insect screens are practical ways to keep insects away from outdoor sensory spaces and make a space inviting, giving the surroundings a hazy, filtered ambience, subtly blurring the view and muting colours and shapes.

Mosquito nets can be hung in doorways to create a breezy walkway; used to enclose a space for a calm area; draped as ceiling décor; wrapped around posts or pillars for a softened and decorative effect; placed over hammocks; combined with other fabrics to create layered textures; used to diffuse sunlight; and draped over a hoop or rail to make a tent.

Using Insect Screens

Carol (childminder from Cheshire)

I use insect screens as doors over my homemade tents when the children in my care are enjoying an outdoor picnic, as they keep the wasps away. Insect screens are the perfect barrier between the indoors and outdoors, allowing the children to see, hear, listen to and smell the natural world through a screen.

N Net Curtains

Whereas mosquito nets are made of a light, fine mesh, allowing airflow, net curtains are more decorative and allow more light to filter through while sill preserving privacy. The material is semi-transparent, with patterned embroidery or lacework. Net curtains can be attached to or draped over a frame, gazebo, tent or marquee. 'Add a variety of textures and sparkle in the form of lights, tinsel and lametta to create a magical feel,' writes **Sarah Hall**, founder of **Willows Sensory Service**, who created a Winter Wonderland made from net curtains.

Winter Wonderland

Sarah Hall

Blocking out some of the external environment is calming and like entering another world. White material is great if you have a light effect to use with it – for example, a mirror ball or mirror ball torch or a Christmas snow projector.

I created a Winter Wonderland sensory drama in school. I hung material – white sheets, mosquito nets, net curtains, shower curtains, baby blankets, towels and tablecloths – from a frame using cup hooks and covered the flooring in white tactile rugs.

The branches were bought ones with little 'jewels' entwined but would be easy enough to make. The addition of a sensory tree would enhance this idea.

FIGURE N.1 Winter Wonderland tent.
Photograph by Sarah Hall

O Observation Windows

A chair or seating area by a window lets in natural light and offers a visual connection to outside activities and nature, creating a peaceful yet engaging space which is perfect for relaxing and observing the world around you.

Select a door or window that offers a view of a landscape or gardens. Install a window bird feeder or butterfly or squirrel feeding station; or plant wildflower seeds in a tub or stack of tyres.

If you don't have a garden area, opt for a spot with a clear view of the sky to watch passing planes, flying birds or the changing weather. Enhance the area by strategically installing wind chimes, suncatchers, a water feature, windsocks or windmills.

Furnish the area using comfortable seating and decorative elements such as plants and artworks. Provide access to binoculars, a camera, a notebook and pen and nature guides.

O Outdoor Spaces

Visiting outdoor spaces offers a rich sensory experience, facilitates social interactions and enables people to connect with nature in an ever-changing landscape.

Visit beaches, botanical gardens, campgrounds, community gardens, farms, fields, forests, greenhouses, hiking trails, lakeshores, meadows, mountains, national parks, nature reserves, orchards, parks and picnic areas.

Ralph Booker, formerly autism training director at **Hampshire Autistic Society** (1996-2008), explains that one popular day service and residential activity was walking as a group to the beach at Stokes Bay, with its natural source of sensory treats: kelp, rockpools, all manner of shells and wildlife (crabs, eels, small fish, starfish), and the feeling of sand, pebbles and the waves on bare feet.

Here **Gerard Wainwright**, a learning disability nurse and founder of **The Unsafe Swallow Project**, writes about sharing sensory opportunities in nature.

Sharing Sensory Opportunities in Nature

Gerard Wainwright

The natural world is abundant with sensory treasures and a gift to share with sensory beings.

Being Receptive to Sensory Opportunities in Nature

We are surrounded by nature. It's free to access and belongs to us all. Even in urban spaces, parks, gardens, canal walks, trees and grass verges can easily be found. If you're in a carpark or concrete jungle, just look up and you'll be rewarded by the endlessly fascinating and often dramatic sky.

All Weather is a Sensory Opportunity

Our national obsession is *the weather*. We characteristically object to it being too wet, too dry, too cold, too hot ... as if the weather is in opposition to our relationship with the outdoors. As a sensory opportunity, our diverse climate is a friend to the senses. Every cloud may not have a silver lining, but it does have the promise of rain, wind and changes to the light and atmosphere.

Nature's Touch

Most people appreciate the kiss of the sun on their skin; but the drama of a changing sky, the invigorating pleasure of a downpour, being buffeted by wind or the nip of frost can be equally inspiring. The sense of feeling part of and immersed in the forces of nature is to feel alive.

Safely Supporting Growth and Exploration

With some planning, nature can be experienced safely, with dramatic benefits for our health and wellbeing. Not everyone will be able to scale the highest peak or swim in the ocean, but that shouldn't exclude us from the everyday miracles of the natural world.

Bringing Nature Indoors

> *To see a World in a Grain of Sand*
> *And a Heaven in a Wild Flower,*
> *Hold Infinity in the palm of your hand*

William Blake

If a person can't go to nature, bring nature to them – shells, feathers, pebbles, acorns, a blade of grass ... Accessible sensory experiences to press, hold, touch, smell, see and experience firsthand.

FIGURE O.1 Looking out over Norland Moor.
Photograph by Gerard Wainwright

P Parachutes

Parachute activities are a popular form of physical, sensory and recreational therapy, creating a supportive environment for interaction, fostering a sense of teamwork and cooperation and building communication skills.

The parachute provides sensory feedback through the sensation of the silky fabric against the skin and the rustling sounds and airflow it creates as it moves. Its size and vibrant colours capture attention.

Drape over a chair or wheelchair to create an inviting space or construct an open parachute tent by securing it to a wall or ceiling. For a closed parachute tent, gather a group of people around a parachute laid on the ground. Together, lift and hold up the parachute to form a dome, release and enjoy the sheltered space.

TACPAC and Music Parachute

Christy Townson, SEN teacher, Hillside Specialist School and College

We use a parachute as a large tent in which students can listen to music and in which the team delivers massage and TACPAC.

P Parasols

Larger than a standard umbrella, parasols are designed to provide shade from the sun. Many have advanced sun protection technology, including UV-blocking materials, cooling properties and moisture-wicking fabrics.

Parasols can be used indoors secured on a parasol base or outdoors using a base or placed directly into soil, grass or thick sand.

Moira Stephens has specialised in assistive technology, PMLD and multisensory impairments for over 35 years. Moira works at Claremont School and independently. She explains here how she used parasols to make festival tents.

Festival Parasols

Moira Stephens

Along with our older students and their parents, we had great fun creating two festival tents out of two huge outdoor parasols and joining them up to make one tent. Both sides were able to comfortably accommodate two students in chairs with support staff.

Each tent had accessible lights and music for ravers or hand and foot massage with accessible calming music for chillout time.

The fabric with handprints and initials was created at a parents' evening. The activity went down well, as it enabled parents and carers to create something with their child and then spend time using it on our festival day.

Sensory spaces can be places for gentle calm and self-regulation or vibrant, engaging areas for immersion in a beautiful sensory whirlwind that stimulates the entire body through the senses.

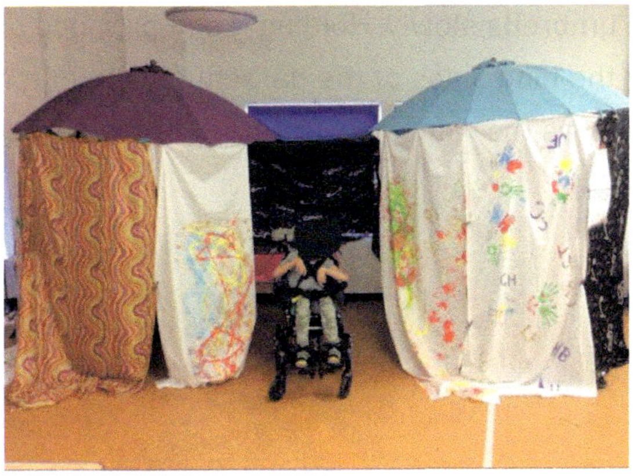

FIGURE P.1 Festival Parasols.
Photograph by Moira Stephens

Claire Graham is the founder of **Inclusion Un.Limited,** which provides sensory activities, music, art and intensive interaction for adults with PMLD in Buckinghamshire. Here she explains how to combine two simple sensory props to make an instant den.

Parachute and Golf Umbrella Tent

Claire Graham

An umbrella and a parachute transform into a quick, easy and effective sensory den.

Draping a brightly coloured parachute over a large white golf umbrella creates an easy-to-hold mini tent, instantly changing your environment and creating a more intimate area to explore.

The structure is easy to move over individuals with different postural needs: we have explored this mini tent sitting down and while people are stretched out in the comfort of their beds.

This sensory space is easy to set up outside on a sunny day, allowing the light to make the colours glow bright against the white of the umbrella. This becomes a fantastic visual and proprioceptive resource as you explore different colours and patterns of materials.

We found that people who were visual sensory seekers enjoyed watching the colours change as we spun the umbrella slowly. Holding it still provided opportunities for individuals to explore moving the long sides of the parachute with different parts of their body; or we could listen intently as the wind blew the sides of the parachute onto us.

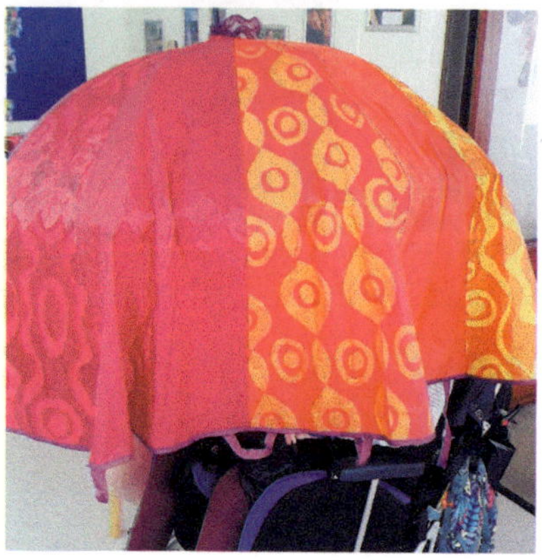

FIGURE P.2 Golf umbrella and parachute tent.
Photograph by Claire Graham

P Partitions and Room Dividers

Room dividers and acoustic partitions are portable and feature lightweight steel frames, making them an ideal base for creating instant spaces, focused learning environments, independent study areas, workstations and quiet zones. For example, you can create a relaxing space by adding items that aid relaxation, headphones to cut out noise or fidget toys to aid self-regulation. The dividers provide privacy and reduce visual distractions, while their sound-absorbing core dulls noise, promoting concentration and engagement.

They can also be used creatively to make tactile structures. **Sophie Davey**, SEN lead at **Manor Green Primary School**, made a bright and tactile 3D coral reef with auditory feedback for students to explore using a classroom divider.

Sophie wrapped the partition in different coloured, UV and textured fabrics and materials, and then attached pompoms, lametta, tinsel and twisted white paper with UV paint to make the coral.

FIGURE P.3 Interactive coral reef.
Photograph by Sophie Davey

P Peg Spinners

A peg spinner is a low-cost item that can easily be transformed into a sensory chandelier by clipping sensory items onto the pegs. The spinner can be held by the facilitator, hooked to a structure or retractable washing line or suspended from a ceiling.

The movement of the peg spinner allows items to be easily explored and provides a soothing effect, promoting relaxation and mindfulness. Visually stimulating chandeliers can be created to reflect light or accessorised with items chosen by the sensory explorer.

Use novelty peg spinners (eg, an octopus as a base for an 'Under the Sea' theme); or create a sensory story by adding props representing characters and events as they appear in the story.

Julie Cowpe-Stephens and Helen Dillon are the founders of **Simply Sensory Training and Support Ltd**. They have many years' experience and expertise working with children and young adults with complex learning, sensory and physical disabilities, within both SEN and mainstream settings. Their rainbow peg spinner is an example of how accessorising a peg spinner with colourful paint and fluorescent paint can stimulate the visual sense for a learner.

Rainbow Peg Spinner

Julie Cowpe-Stephens and Helen Dillon

The person we created the rainbow spinner for has limited movement and needs a lot of bright visual movement to stimulate their visual sense. The peg spinner enabled them to engage and interact with the colours and movement of the paper.

We added fluorescent paint in matching colours to the paper, so the rainbow spinner came to life under a UV light in a darkened room.

The peg spinner can be used indoors or outdoors and can be placed within the learner's reach so that they can independently engage and interact with the rainbow to make it move.

The rainbow peg spinner is wonderful to use outdoors. It can be suspended from a variety of things in the garden within the learner's field of vision, so they can watch the colours move in the breeze. This encourages the learner to attend, fixate and track the rainbow.

FIGURE P.4 Rainbow peg spinner.
Photograph by Simply Sensory Training and Support Ltd

A rainbow peg spinner can also be transformed into a larger space by pulling out the ribbons.

FIGURE P.5 Expanded rainbow peg spinner.
Photograph by Sarah Hall

P Playhouses

Usually made of wood and resembling a miniature house, these structures are a foundation for the sensory spaces. They can be converted into a dark zone for relaxation, accessorised for use as a stimulating sensory exploration area or furnished to make an enriching imaginative play area, encouraging social interaction and cooperation and nurturing social skills and friendships.

Place items inside the playhouse to encourage roleplay or change the room theme (eg, kitchen, lounge). Extend into the space outside the playhouse by laying astroturf and accessorising using pots of fresh flowers and herbs.

Theme the playhouse (eg, 'Vintage' or 'Washing Day'); or create sensory stations inside, adding containers filled with scented items or small boxes to rummage through containing different textured items. Accessorise into an immersive area for exploring topics.

Castor Church of England Primary School adapted their wooden playhouse into an inviting reading nook. Headteacher **Suzie Phillips** tells us more.

Reading Nook

Suzie Phillips

The reading nook in our school serves as a vital resource for students, offering them an opportunity to engage with high-quality texts in a calm and inviting environment. The students have expressed a profound appreciation for this dedicated space, indicating that they feel serene and focused while reading. They not only immerse themselves in stories, but also partake in collaborative sharing, reading to one another and retelling narratives using their own words alongside recently introduced vocabulary.

This process is often facilitated with the use of toys and various resources, making learning both interactive and enjoyable. It encourages students to explore non-fiction literature, rhymes and poems during roleplay activities. This multifaceted approach enhances their comprehension and appreciation of diverse literary forms.

As they progress, children are supported in developing their phonetic skills through sound blending, allowing them to read words aligned with their phonic knowledge.

New vocabulary is consistently added to the reading nook as it is learned, promoting continual growth. Children begin to read aloud simple sentences and books that align with their phonetic abilities, including common exception words.

The main learning outcomes from this initiative are increased literacy skills, enhanced vocabulary and a deeper love of reading, fostering a lifelong appreciation for literature.

FIGURE P.6 Reading nook.
Photograph by Suzie Phillips

P Polytunnels

Polytunnels are primarily used as greenhouses to trap solar heat and create a warmer environment, sheltering plants, fruits and vegetables from the elements in a controlled and protected growing space.

In your home, school or setting, a polytunnel can be used to grow produce to eat, with seeds or plugs planted directly in the ground or in pots. Harvest seeds and sell cuttings, plants and produce. Sunflowers, courgettes, herbs and tomatoes are very easy to grow and always popular.

Plant wildflowers inside your polytunnel to make a butterfly house – ensure you leave an opening for them to freely come and go.

Convert into an outdoor classroom to teach botany, ecology and environmental science. Conduct experiments on plant growth, photosynthesis and the effects of variables, climate control studies, composting and microclimate creation.

Polytunnels can be accessorised for use as calm, enclosed spaces for therapeutic activities, such as mindfulness sessions, yoga or quiet time. They can be customised to create immersive learning environments tailored to specific topics (eg, spring or the jungle), or decorated to celebrate festivals and celebrations.

P Plumbing Pipes and Connectors

Plastic pipes and connectors are affordable, durable and versatile, making them ideal for a wide range of sensory activities. Incorporate into sand and water play to explore concepts such as gravity and buoyancy. Tap, blow and drop items such as dried beans into the pipes to produce different sounds. Attach to light sources (LED lights and torches) for a visual sensory activity or use in small world play as tunnels and roads for toy cars and balls.

Rosie Brister is an independent specialist in PMLD provision and an experienced practitioner of intensive interaction, hydrotherapy and rebound therapy. She was previously lead teacher for pupils with physical and/or sensory impairment.

Rosie's sensory cube is a wonderful example of how everyday items can be creatively repurposed into a sensory structure.

The Sensory Cube

Rosie Brister

I made this sensory cube. It is a freestanding structure, although it is more stable if it is attached to the wall, which I did in my setting. Essentially constructed from plumbing pipes and fittings, it is lightweight and easily moveable and can be packed down if required.

The cube's entrance deliberately did not have a crossbar on the floor to ensure ease of access by anyone using wheeled equipment (pacers/standers/chairs). The height was calculated to ensure that taller learners could still access the area in their standing frames.

The sensory cube was used to enhance opportunities for independent sensory exploration linked to our topic of 'Winter/Cold'.

The addition of a piece of fabric over the front of the cube enabled learners to be completely enclosed in the space, free to explore without distraction. The addition of switch-controlled resources added another level of stimulation to the experience. Fans created movement in the cube, while fairy lights changed the visual aspects within. Music and soundscapes could also be added if required.

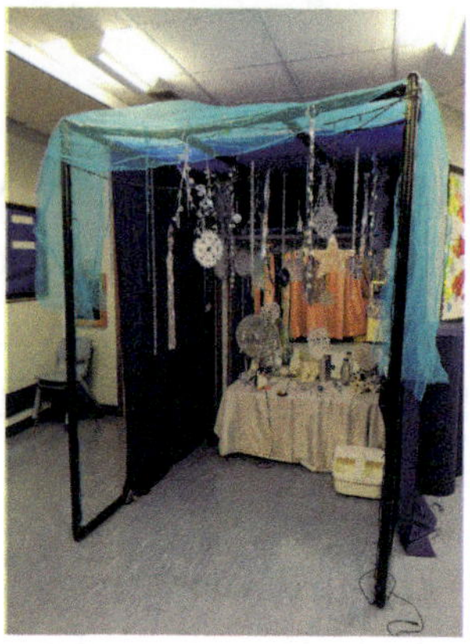

FIGURE P.7 'Winter/Cold' themed sensory cube frame.
Photograph by Rosie Brister

FIGURE P.8 'Winter/Cold' themed sensory cube with accessories.
Photograph by Rosie Brister

Q Quiet Spaces

Create a tranquil space to enjoy peaceful activities such as reading, colouring, working on puzzles, practising yoga, listening to calming music or engaging in mindfulness exercises.

Set the mood with soft, low lighting and comfortable furnishings. Play soothing music or incorporate sound therapy using percussion instruments, chimes, finger cymbals, gongs, shamanic hand drums or singing bowls. Introduce calming scents and soft, tactile items, a yoga mat, massage tools and creams, and natural elements such as potted plants – geraniums, lavender and tomato plants will add a subtle scent to the space. A solar fountain provides a soothing background sound.

AnnMarie Walker spent 25 years as both an SEN teacher and senior leader before taking her skills in a different direction by becoming a psychotherapist. Here she shares five ways to incorporate mindfulness practice into the classroom.

Incorporating Mindfulness into Sensory Work

AnnMarie Walker

Learning the skills of mindfulness allows us to develop strategies to help keep us in the moment and calm anxieties, stresses or worries that we may have. We all practise some of these skills without realising – for example, taking a big breath before saying something that may be difficult. Learning to control our breathing is one of the key processes within mindfulness.

Mindfulness is about being present in the here and now and being aware of ourselves and our surroundings in the moment. It can help children to feel and understand their emotions before reacting, which supports their emotional regulation and development of emotional awareness.

The more we teach our young people mindfulness practice, the more automatic it will become for them, helping them become less anxious and more emotionally intelligent.

Create a Den that is Zen

Sometimes the classroom and wider school environment can be overwhelming for children as their senses are overloaded. A space that allows them to reset their overwhelmed mind helps regulate them back to their baseline level, enabling them to re-engage with their learning.

Ideally, this would be a small room that is permanently set up; however, if space is at a premium, a dark den/tent in the corner of the classroom will also work. Accessorise using soft cushions or a seated beanbag, a rug, a calming light source (eg, a push-button, battery-operated light if electrical resources are not an option), a blanket, a music source (eg, wireless speaker) playing instrumental music, a projection light and a timer.

Have some small objects to hand that encourage slow breathing: feathers to blow, a toy windmill or a bubble wand will naturally support the child to regulate their breathing. You may also want some small fidget toys; you can add whatever is suitable depending on the interests of the child, but refrain from making the space cluttered.

Immersive Environment and a Mindful Journey

If you are fortunate to have a fully immersive space in your school, complete with projection, sound and lights, this would be ideal for activities such as this. If you don't, you can create your own as suggested here.

Immersing all of our senses into one experience helps gives us a sense of calm, awe and wonder. For some children, simply being in the space and exploring their senses will be an appropriate use, allowing them to focus on the input into their own bodies. For others, you can use the environment you have created to take them on a mindful journey– a type of meditation practice where the participant is guided through a scenario in their mind's eye. This works best for children who can remain still and listen for a short period: they can fully focus on the journey, seeing, hearing and feelings things that are described along the way. This helps them become centred within themselves and concentrate on their internal and external feelings.

If you are unable to access an empty, bright space, then using a large white tent or blocking off a corner using white sheets can also work. Decide on the theme of the immersion – for example, 'In the Forest' or 'In a Snowstorm'.

Suggested Props

- **Sight:** Projection of pictures relating to your theme (an iPad and small projector can be used for this) and objects relating to your theme (eg, soft toys, sensory materials).
- **Sound:** Appropriate sounds relating to your theme (eg, birdsong for 'In the Forest'). Sound files and clips can be downloaded and played through speakers.
- **Touch:** Sensory objects that match your theme (eg, a tray of sand for 'At the Beach' or leaves for 'In the Forest').

- **Smell and taste:** Activities relating to smell and taste may be appropriate for the room if the children are exploring it themselves; however, sound and touch activities are the most useful for the mindful journey. Encourage them to sit or lie on a mat while you take them through a mindful journey based on your theme. There are commercially produced examples of these covering a range of themes; otherwise, you can have fun creating your own.

Mindfulness in Nature

Being outdoors improves mood, helps us feel more relaxed, supports our ability to focus and concentrate and gives us a sense of joy. Making use of the outdoor spaces that are available to you is hugely beneficial.

The resources you have for this activity will very much depend on the available outdoor space. Whether a grassy field, some trees along the boundary line, a sandpit, a sensory garden or a gravel playground, all outdoor spaces allow for exploration and mindfulness work. Being mindful in the natural environment means encouraging the children to use their senses to be present. Listen to the crunch of leaves or shoes on gravel; feel springy grass underfoot or the hardness of branches on their hands; see the different colours that surround them.

For some children, the use of visual prompts can support them to focus. For example, have some picture cards of objects you would like them to find and explore, if they need help to engage.

Mindfulness Colouring – Large Scale

Mindfulness colouring is beneficial in a number of ways. It reduces stress and anxiety and helps us focus on the here and now and what is happening at this point, rather than being drawn into the past or future.

There are many commercial or printable small-scale resources available which you can place in a calm corner or zen den. Mindfulness colouring on a large scale requires bigger movements and a larger area to focus on. Use a large chalkboard or flipchart, attached to a wall either inside or outside of the classroom. On the surface, either pre-draw or encourage the children to create different lines and spaces on the surface with either black or white media (depending on whether you are using paper or a chalkboard). Then, using whatever media the child enjoys – crayons, pens, paint – they can focus on colouring in the small spaces they have created.

R Rails

Secure a towel rail to the wall or accessorise a portable garment hanging rail to create an interactive sensory station. Adjust the height to accommodate wheelchair and standing frame users. Increase the space by hanging a fabric shoe holder from the rail and placing items inside the compartments. Two-tiered garment rails often include shelves and racks, increasing storage capacity.

Tie objects to the rail that encourage sensory exploration and engagement. Focus on one sense at a time – for example, create a tactile rail by filling little cloth bags with dried rice, beans, pulses or flour to add weight; or add gel beads that can be squeezed and manipulated.

Theme your rail – for example, for a farm-themed rail, hang fruits, vegetables, an egg-shaped musical shaker, feathers, wool, a bundle of fresh straw, toy animals, bags of seeds and grains, and dried corn cobs.

The rail in Figure R.1 was made by **Debbie Delahaye** for Sapphire Class at **Meadowfield School** in Kent.

Making a Sensory Rail

Debbie Delahaye and team

Sensory rails are designed to be accessible to pupils and meet their sensory preferences. Each element included provides different sensory feedback: visual, tactile and auditory. These elements elicit a different response from pupils and open up further opportunities for communication, such as commenting, 'So shiny!' or 'Like'/'Don't like.'

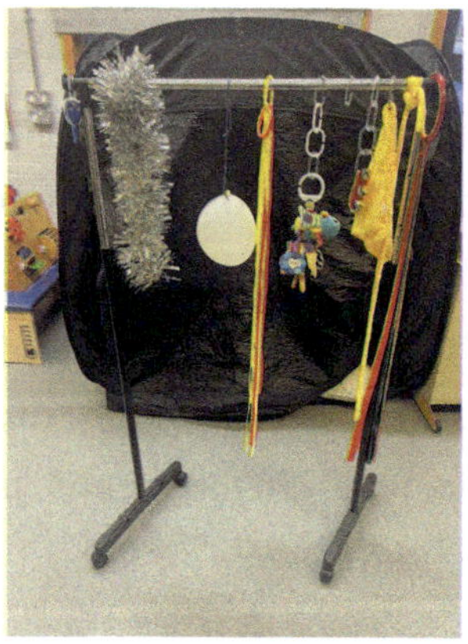

FIGURE R.1 Sensory rail.
Photograph by Debbie Delahaye

R Remote Interactive Learning Experiences

A remote interactive learning experience is where the participant engages in stories or activities via the internet, instead of attending a session or class in person. There are lots of platforms to tap into, giving people a chance to be a part of something even if they are restricted by being at home or in hospital.

Sophie Kidd-Munnery is a dedicated mum to Maisy and Poppy. Maisy was one of more than 700 participants aged between three and 18-plus who joined a live interactive sensory storytelling session I held to celebrate World Book Day 2025.

Prior to the event, facilitators were sent a list of props with guidance for prop delivery. I delivered the story live via Zoom using a PowerPoint presentation, pausing in between slides to allow time for sensory exploration.

Remote and Virtual Interactive Learning Experiences

Sophie Kidd-Munnery

I have experience running sensory storytelling sessions. This was a lovely time in my life as I met a very special lady called Suzanne – an incredible individual who helped everyone in the community and took on Maisy's fundraising. Suzanne became a soulmate and took me under her wing, opening up an opportunity for me to hold sensory story sessions in the community library that she ran. I do this all the time for my girls, who love my stories. I wanted to share my knowledge and it gave me another purpose, as Suzanne enabled me to believe in myself.

Very sadly, Suzanne passed away during the pandemic. I hold onto those memories of my friend. We called her Maisy's 'Fairy Godmother'; Suzanne genuinely cared about us as a family.

The live interactive sensory storytelling session held by Victoria Navin, the founder of Rhyming Multisensory Stories, was a celebration of books. Maisy's sister Poppy helped with the props, along with me and Auntie Helena, who also helps care for Maisy.

Maisy enjoyed the tinkling sound of the wind chimes as story participants were welcomed into a magic place. We used a guiro and stick to represent knocking at the library door. We met various characters throughout the story. A caterpillar was represented by a moving, tactile slug fidget toy that makes a sound, adding an auditory value.

Poppy held a black cape decorated with a stars and moon pattern to recreate the darkness of a bear's cave. My sister had the idea of placing a fan behind the material as we projected light from a handheld starlight projector onto it, to make it shimmer. Portable projectors are easier to put into different positions for Maisy. Maisy is registered blind but sometimes we observe a slight connection. You can see in Figure R.2 that this was one of those rare moments, as the movement of the tiny pieces of glitter inside the projector caught Maisy's attention for a split second and we saw a visual response, which was lovely. We used a torch to look for the hidden bear.

We shook a cabasa percussion instrument to represent a train (Maisy is responsive to sound). Cool, white, satin material combined with a glitter projector became a sparkling, snowy sky.

We beat an African drum to replicate the heartbeat of Jack on his adventures up the beanstalk, and I did chest percussions in time. We were all dressed up as characters from *Charlie and the Chocolate Factory*, as it was World Book Day. Maisy wore a chocolate bar outfit; Poppy dressed up as Willy Wonka, wearing his top hat, which we used as a prop within the story; and I went all-out and bought Oompa-Loompa outfits for myself and my sister – it's always nice to get involved yourself! Maisy finds the whole sensory experience so much more enjoyable and stimulating when we all participate.

For the non-fiction elements of the story, a musical instrument pod with shells and netting recreated the sounds of the rainforest. We used different tools for tapping and scraping and ran our fingers along it, feeling the vibrations and the beat.

Maisy ran her hands up and down the fabric of a gold-coloured, sequined pillowcase representing the gritty sensation of the desert sand. A roaring tiger sound clip played on a phone brought our tiger-shaped giggle stick to life. We blasted off into space with balls of different textures representing the planets, and with a hot water bottle radiating the heat from Mars.

Outcomes

The remote interactive sensory story created an immersive experience for Maisy. It was a lovely opportunity for her to participate in something tailored to her and her needs, and for us to be part of that journey with her. It was great the sensory story was delivered on

World Book Day, as we were celebrating. I liked the repetition of the session: it was well put together, with simple sentences, enabling us to recreate the moment and capture the story.

We are not sure how much Maisy is aware of what we are doing, but we know for certain she picks up on when we immerse ourselves in the activity with her – that's the beauty of it, and that's when those special moments happen. At the start of the story, Maisy was quite sleepy, but she came to life responding to it.

Maisy is often housebound, so the virtual sessions make up her life now – this was a positive that came out of the pandemic. Maisy loves the Marvin Story Show and for my own progression, I completed the training for the Story Massage Programme.

I love being part of the networking. The world should be like that – people supporting each other; I think the pandemic encouraged this. It's nice to be part of a bigger community and make connections, even if it is through a screen. We call them our virtual friends, even though we have never met.

I like to share my experiences and journey with Maisy. She has taught us so much and we have submerged ourselves in her world as much as we possibly can. There are bad times, such as when she is poorly; but people like Victoria Navin, Mary Atkinson from the Story Massage Programme, Gwyn McCormack from Marvin's Storytime Show and others take a real interest in providing opportunities for us to forget about the bad things for a bit and enable Maisy to be part of something special and bring the outside world inside for her.

Some people may be cautious of remote sessions, but I feel people may be missing out on that side of it if they aren't willing to explore. I would urge them to explore the virtual options and give them a go: get involved yourself and create some very special memories together.

FIGURE R.2 Maisy inside the 'bear's cave'.
Photograph by Sophie Kidd-Munnery

S Sandpits

Sand provides sensory feedback and opportunities to explore, learn and develop cognitive, physical and social skills, as children collaborate and play together. Using sand tools for digging, scooping, sifting and pouring the sand builds hand-eye coordination and fine motor and problem-solving skills. Imaginative play in the sand enhances language and communication skills.

To create an all-weather station outdoors, place a tarpaulin over a sandpit. For indoor settings, placing sand inside a pop-up tent or inflatable swimming pool creates a safe space for exploration while containing the sand within the area, which can be easily cleaned by shaking it outdoors or vacuuming after the activity.

Explore the properties of wet and dry sand. Make sensory sand by adding flour, oil or glitter; or dye the sand using food colouring for a vibrant effect. Incorporate topics, themes and small world play activities: create an archaeological dig; recreate habitats, deserts, riverbanks and beaches; set up a treasure hunt; explore mathematical concepts (measurement, capacity); or draw patterns using combs and sticks.

On a larger scale, create a building site roleplay area by providing hard hats, high-visibility jackets, goggles, cones, plastic shovels, spades and small wheelbarrows; and mix grey powder paint with flour and sand to make 'cement'.

Emma Pauley's youngest daughter Millie was born with a very rare genetic condition called TUBA1a. Here Emma shares her ideas for weaving sensory experiences into daily routines.

Making a Sandbox

Emma Pauley and daughter Millie

We have a sandbox with hidden treasures such as foam letters and beads in it. This is super-messy, but it's something Millie will sit and play with for ages. It's great to encourage her to do tasks such as finding certain letters or coloured items.

Sandpits/trays are very effective placed inside sensory spaces. Using a sand tray in a dark tent creates a unique and engaging sensory environment, as demonstrated by the EYFS Department at **Meadowfield School** in Kent.

Using a Sand Tray in a Dark Tent

EYFS Department, Meadowfield School

We placed our sand tray inside a tent, which provided a calming space and a controlled environment with minimal distractions.

This facilitated a motivating and engaging activity linked to a seaside theme, which was used to develop communication and interaction in a hands-on, practical way in a low-demand environment. This prepared the pupils for a visit to the beach.

The sand toys and shells promote fine motor skills development, inviting students to explore.

FIGURE S.1 A sensory sand tray inside a tent.
Photograph by the EYFS Department, Meadowfield School

Peter Imray is a freelance trainer, adviser and writer on SEN and director of developments at **EQUALS**. Here Peter explains how, using the Principles of Play outlined in the EQUALS curriculum, we can bring the beach to the school.

Taking the Seaside to the Classroom

Peter Imray

Anyone who has seen children playing on a beach will know that all you need for hours of engaging, interactive, exploring, learning FUN is sand, water and as many shovels, spades, buckets and pourers as the children can handle.

BIG IS BETTER! The amount of sand and water on a beach is unlimited and one of the joys of playing at the seaside is that children don't run out of resources. We must think in terms of providing LOTS of sand and LOTS of water; and, for as long as the play is going on, replacing sand and water as soon as they are shovelled, poured, tipped, spilt, thrown. So, BIG builder's trays on stands – for older learners, shop at a builders' suppliers. The bigger they are and the more they have in them, the more they allow numerous children to play at the same play station. The children might or might not be playing cooperatively; but they'll never learn to if the resources offered are measly and rationed.

One way to ensure that water is always interesting is to make it run. Place a large, deep tub outside and put a simple solar-powered pump at the bottom, weighted down to ensure no one takes it out. The pump can act as a fountain; or, even better, you could make a slalom effect with lengths of guttering. Just make sure the water is replaced every day with fresh, warm water, especially in the colder months.

S Sensory Rooms

Sensory rooms support people with their sensory processing through multisensory stimulation. Depending on the size of your room and budget, key features may include olfactory items (eg, oil diffusers and scented items); equipment to promote proprioceptive and vestibular stimulation (eg, balance beams and boards, body socks, crash mats, foam rollers, scooter boards, sensory paths, stepping stones, swings, therapy balls, trampettes and tunnels); and tactile items (eg, sensory bins or touch stations).

Sensory rooms can also be used for adventures, as the following case study based on my work with a Year 4 SEN student demonstrates.

CASE STUDY: SHARK ISLAND SENSORY ROOM

Aim

To engage Student A, who needed additional encouragement to participate in his sensory diet programme.

Background

I used the STICKIDS software and activity kit, which provides therapeutic strategies through visual aids, activities and sensory diets to support students with their sensory processing and integration, and to aid self-regulation. The sensory room was timetabled for Student A's individual sessions.

Student A did not like the formality and routine of a structured programme: when offered a choice of different activities, he would shake his head and choose to lie on the beanbag instead.

Materials and Resources

The room had a padded floor and walls and was equipped with proprioceptive and vestibular equipment and sensory items.

Implementation

To make the session motivating, I used the equipment in the room to create adventures incorporating the activities into Student A's plan. His favourite story was 'Shark Island'. He engaged in his heavy work activities by lifting and carrying the giant foam shapes to create the land and laying out blue crash mats on the floor to represent the sea. He caught small beanbags I threw and placed them on the mats to represent sharks. He navigated his obstacle course, bouncing off a trampette to avoid falling in the water and being 'eaten' by the sharks. He 'walked the plank' using a balance board; a scooter board became the ship; resistance bands served as oars; and the spinning sensory cone represented the swirling sea.

I hid 'treasure' under the foam shapes and beanbags and on the top ledges of the soft padded walls to encourage him to climb and stretch.

Challenges and Solutions

The main challenge was the scheduling of the room, as it was timetabled for one-to-one sensory sessions. To address this, I incorporated a story-based approach with a structured yet flexible framework and a clear ending. After completing Student A's sensory diet activities, I used a five-minute sand timer to transition to a calming session. We dimmed the lights, sat on large beanbags and listened to the sound of the rainmaker while he explored the colourful patterns changing as he rotated the dial on the kaleidoscope, using it as a telescope to check the pirates had sailed away into the distance.

Impact

This personalised approach led to significant improvements in Student A's coordination, cognitive skills, social interaction, communication, independence, emotional stability and overall confidence.

I extended this model into lunch breaks, taking it to the outdoor area where Student A could play out the stories with peers, further enhancing engagement and social interaction.

Conclusion

The implementation of a story used with sensory circuits for students with sensory processing disorder significantly improved sensory regulation, motor skills and focus and promoted emotional stability, social interaction and overall wellbeing, highlighting its value in educational settings.

From 1996-2008, **Ralph Booker** was the autism training director at **Hampshire Autistic Society**, where he worked with Ron 'Nobby' Clark, head of day services. Ralph shares his memories of the sensory room at the ADS.

Sensory Rooms

Ralph Booker

The main emphasis of the sensory room was to encourage relaxation, stimulation and sharing, since some resources could only be used one person at a time and sharing – a social activity – can be difficult for some autistic people. The room was large enough to accommodate four users at a time with one or two staff in support. The room used fluorescent light, mild sounds, textures (eg, seashells) and heat (eg, rice bags). The room had deckchairs and a beanbag so users could take a passive role and simply relax, and colours and sounds changed. Others could walk around.

S Shower Curtains

Shower curtains are a cheap, lightweight tool for making sensory spaces. Their built-in loops can be threaded onto a rail or a hula hoop. Being waterproof, they are easy to clean and fold away for storage when not in use. Shower curtains are available in many different designs and patterns, providing instant backdrops for themes or topics, such as alphabet (literacy), aquarium or dinosaurs.

The waterproof fabric of shower curtains ensures they can withstand light rain showers when used outdoors. They can be easily secured to structures such as fences, railings or trees with rope, providing shelter or sensory spaces while offering shade from the sun. They also serve as a perfect backdrop for projecting images.

FIGURE S.2 Image projected onto a shower curtain for a festival day for charity Solo. Photograph by Sarah Hall

S Side Lyers

A side lyer is a positioning aid used to provide support and gentle pressure to the body, affording a sense of comfort and security.

When designing a sensory space using a side lyer, ensure it provides adequate support and consider the individual's sensory preferences. Some people prefer firm support; others prefer soft, with the option to add blankets and cushions.

Pauline Woodcock, a SEN teacher at **Fairfield School**, created a sensory space using a side lyer, a disco ball and two umbrellas – one black and one white, to create a contrast.

Black and White Disco Ball Golf Umbrella and Side Lyer

Pauline Woodcock

I use large golf umbrellas to create an enclosed visual work area that is portable and can be taken to wherever the student is working. I find this particularly useful when students are doing physiotherapy in standers or on the side lyer.

The individual work zone minimises disruptions from elsewhere in the room. Using the umbrellas enables the student to continue working on their visual skills while maintaining and developing their physical skills.

I use black and white umbrellas; both create an individual work zone but give different visual effects depending on which colour is used. Project light onto a black background and the colour absorbs most of the light, highlighting the bright and colourful lights in a bold and striking way. Projecting light onto a white background generates a softer effect, as the white background umbrella reflects and diffuses the light evenly across the surface, creating a gentle and dreamy atmosphere.

My students especially enjoy working on cause-and-effect skills using the disco ball connected to a switch reflected off the black umbrella. The umbrella intensifies the light and therefore reinforces the learning, encouraging the student to continue working on the activity.

FIGURE S.3 White golf umbrella, disco ball and side lyer.
Photograph by Pauline Woodcock

S Scrim Nets

Scrim nets are versatile: they can be suspended from walls and ceilings or draped over structures to create a soft, diffused light. Hang items that produce natural sounds, windchimes and shells from the scrim net to bring an element of tranquillity and harmony to the space. Create a sensory wall, a mini obstacle course, a backdrop for shadow play using torches or a prop for a sensory story. Promote fine motor skills by using a scrim net as a base for weaving fabric strips through.

Peter Blaker is a qualified teacher currently working with adults living with PMLD. Immersive sensory drama is one of the approaches he loves to use and there are lots of ideas on his **Starfish** Facebook page.

Peter draped a scrim net over a wheelchair to recreate the Hundred Acre Wood in *Winnie the Pooh*.

Recreating the Hundred-Acre Wood

Peter Blaker

A shelter made from camouflage netting formed part of a Winnie the Pooh immersive drama. Hiding inside, with the room darkened and soft music playing, we could see colourful sparkles from our sensory lights twinkling through the netting, like stars in the night forest.

The close, intimate nature of the space provided a tranquil alternative to the lively sensory activities that formed the rest of the story that we had shared outside the shelter. We felt safe and contained; everybody's voices became hushed. We were not hiding from the outside; it felt that, for a short time, we had stepped into a completely different world.

The darkness inside was the perfect place to play with fairy lights and small torches, bringing the leaves of the netting to life by making shadows dance all around us. Fabric leaves in autumn colours were explored, handled and dropped, allowing them to drift to our forest floor.

This was sensory immersion – a place where emotional responses to non-verbal storytelling became real and the characters of Christopher Robin and his friends sprang to life inside the world we created.

S Space Blankets

Space blankets, also known as emergency blankets or survival blankets, can be used creatively to make sensory spaces. Lay them on the floor to enjoy the warm, reflective, crinkly surface. Use as a sunshade, a component of a tent or in a nature hide to attract wildlife.

Here **Richard Hirstwood**, the director **of Hirstwood Training Ltd**, shares his ideas for using space blankets.

Five Ideas for Using Space Blankets

Richard Hirstwood

- Encourage learners to crunch or crinkle the space blanket to develop cause-and-effect awareness, using a unique sound for sensory exploration.
- Space blankets are excellent sensory tools that reflect and spread coloured light over a wide area. Shine coloured torches onto the reflective surface of the space blanket to create vibrant, engaging visual effects.
- Use a bright white torch to reflect a sharp light off the space blanket to gain visual attention.
- Place the space blanket over various textured objects, allowing learners to feel the sensation of different textures through the reflective material.
- Wrap the space blanket loosely around the learner to provide a gentle, crinkling sound and soft sensory feedback as they move.

Rosie Brister is an independent specialist in PMLD provision and an experienced practitioner of intensive interaction, hydrotherapy and rebound therapy. Rosie's previous role was lead teacher for pupils with physical and/or sensory impairment.

Rosie views sensory spaces as invaluable multifaceted learning environments, providing an immersive experience to enhance subject delivery.

Rosie created a suspended hoop with a space blanket to provide either a stimulating interactive space or a calming enclosed area to shelter students from the hustle and bustle of a busy environment.

Suspended Hoop with Space Blanket

Rosie Brister

The suspended hoop with a space blanket wrap was a prototype made in response to an observation by Dr Joanna Grace about the value of providing accessible activities to learners who often have to wait for adult assistance to enable them to access their immediate environment.

The hoop was rigged on a pulley system so that it could be lowered for learners having time out from their equipment on the floor. Battery-powered fairy lights were installed and looked great reflecting off the silver cover when the room lights were dimmed. A large bangle was tied to the hoop via a ribbon that could be placed within reach of the learner to enable them to hold onto and move the resource. If they were unable to hold the bangle, it could be placed on the wrist or ankle to facilitate independent access through gross motor movement instead.

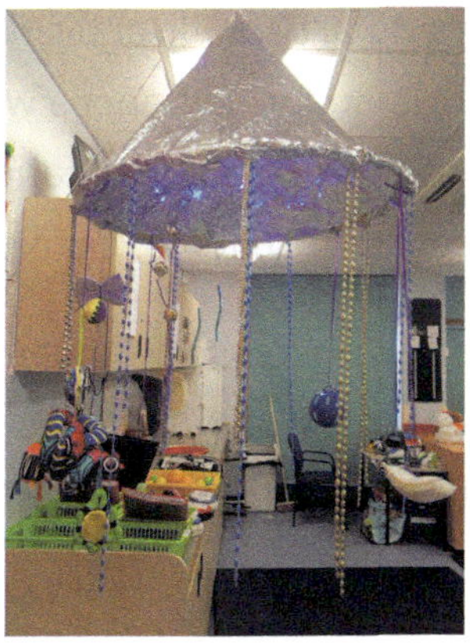

FIGURE S.4 Suspended hoop with space blanket.
Photograph by Rosie Brister

S Stages

Transforming a stage into a sensory space offers a stimulating environment tailored to meet sensory needs and enhance learning experiences.

I was contacted by a school for ideas on inclusive ways to involve PMLD students in their Christmas school play. I adapted a sensory story called 'Dear Santa' based on a poem my late Dad wrote and included a walk-through of a mini play based on the poem with roles for everyone. (This is a free resource to download from www.rhymingmultisensorystories.com.)

Many stages already have lighting systems and auditory equipment in place, so with the addition of props and costumes, you can build a stimulating sensory space.

Make a small stage in a corner of a room using an adjustable shower rail and shower curtains, a mini projector light or glitter ball and a microphone. Add props to stimulate the imagination.

Daniel Swift MBE is chief executive and artistic director of **Concrete Youth**, a charity dedicated to increasing cultural provision for audiences with PMLD through the delivery of sensory theatre productions across the UK. Its education department provides sensory stories, workshops and story massages in schools, care settings and community spaces.

In 2024, Concrete Youth made history with *Sensory Cinders* at **@sohoplace**, the first West End production designed exclusively for PMLD audiences, demonstrating the feasibility of adapting non-traditional spaces into fully immersive theatre environments.

Sensory Theatre

Daniel Swift MBE

Mounting *Sensory Cinders* presented unique challenges, including navigating the commercial theatre sector as a subsidised company and adapting a West End model – typically catering to large audiences – to performances for just six attendees. One of the most significant challenges was the physical space itself.

@sohoplace were exceptional to work with. Their team, the building and their support and passion for the production were all fantastic. However, to ensure the intimacy and interactivity that sensory theatre requires, the production needed to run in their rehearsal room, rather than the main house, requiring a full transformation into an immersive theatre space.

Through a collaborative effort with the team, the space was transformed into a fully immersive theatre environment. The set design incorporated a range of sensory elements, carefully curated to engage audiences labelled with PMLD. A large, textured tree served as the focal point of the space (complete with glowing fungi and pumpkins), providing both a visual and tactile stimulus. The throne, draped in rich fabrics, was designed to be inviting and interactive; while disco balls and shimmering materials hanging throughout the space tied the aesthetic of the show together in the most sensory way possible.

A truss structure supported the technical elements, allowing for an adaptable performance space with ambitious and inclusive lighting design. The lighting design was meticulously planned to provide atmospheric and functional accessibility. The speaker system was programmed to deliver carefully balanced soundscapes, avoiding overwhelming sensory input while maintaining an immersive auditory experience.

To further support audience comfort, a sensory breakout area was established adjacent to the studio, featuring familiar set pieces and interactive elements. @sohoplace staff received specialist training from Concrete Youth, ensuring they could confidently support audience members and contribute to an accessible, welcoming experience throughout the production's run. This was complete with key signs to communicate with and support audiences labelled with PMLD throughout their visit to the theatre.

The production not only was a ground-breaking cultural experience for audiences labelled with PMLD but also demonstrated the feasibility of adapting non-traditional spaces into fully immersive theatre environments. It marked a significant shift in the West End's engagement with inclusive practice for learning disabled audiences and set a precedent for future accessible productions in mainstream theatre for audiences labelled with PMLD.

FIGURE S.5 Ellana Gilbert playing Cinders in the West End Production of *Sensory Cinders* – a Concrete Youth and Barnsley Civic Co-production.

Photograph by Shona Louise

T Tents

Tents can be used indoors and outdoors. The act of erecting a tent is a lesson in itself, presenting an opportunity to learn different skills, from teamwork to critical thinking. Cut the bottom and slip over a chair, wheelchair or standing frame.

A-frame Tents

A-frame tents generally have a triangular shape supported by a central pole. This design is easy to set up and provides good stability in windy conditions, making it ideal for outdoor use.

Blackout Tents

Blackout tents made from material that blocks light can reduce sensory overload. Place light-up resources inside to create a portable light room on a budget, as demonstrated by **The Ark Childcare** (Retford) (see Figure T.1).

FIGURE T.1 Exploring light in the dark tent.
Photograph by The Ark Childcare

Blackout tents are a great tool for sensory storytelling. Here, **Pete Wells** – award-winning SEN teacher and senior leader in the educational sector, writing inclusive stories for **HelpKidzLearn** – shares ideas on incorporating a blackout tent with sensory stories.

Blackout Tents and Inclusive Storytelling

Pete Wells

Oh, how I love a blackout tent – a truly magical area of any classroom! These fantastic spaces are perfect for story explorers to have some regulation time, particularly those who may be overstimulated. Conversely, they act as cool little dens to take part in some wondrous, cosy, concentrated sensory stimulation. Every classroom should have a few!

I particularly like to use them as part of, you guessed it, a sensory story! Vestibular activities are often neglected in sensory storytelling, so for more ambulant learners, having to go into a blackout tent as part of a story can be extremely motivating – and even a little scary! Of course, once you're in there, you need something cool to do (read on for further ideas). However, it's worth noting that if the transition to them is not handled well, they can be very distracting. Many of our story explorers, particularly those with mobility issues, can find it troublesome getting in and out of them, so avoid if transferring to them messes up your story flow.

Thinking of my inclusive stories, a blackout tent has been used effectively for the following activities (and more):

- Imagine diving under the sea with paper plate tropical fish (painted by my story explorers) suspended from the ceiling. 'Millie the Mermaid Who Couldn't Swim' would feel right at home!
- A Limpet Cave, complete with fluorescent paper bowl limpets, sets the stage for the mysterious encounter of 'Millie and the Sirens'.
- Outer space twinkles with fluorescent stars and tinfoil planets, hosting 'The Cutest Little Alien'.
- How about Nessie's Lair, complete with bagpipe music on a single switch communicator and switch-adapted spooky eye torches to bring to life?
- Webster Witch's messy castle becomes a sensory treasure hunt with weather-themed items in 'Webster Witch's Wacky Weather'.
- A Himalayan cave, filled with snowy wadding, ice blue ribbons and tasty ice cream, transports us to 'The Day I Met the Yeti'.
- 'Sir Pranceabout and the Dragon' find refuge in the dragon's cave, complete with IKEA Minnen Drake dragons.
- And, of course, who could forget Sheldon the Snail's ill-fated night-time beach visit, marked by neon stars and a soothing ocean drum? 'Oh slime!'

The tents needn't just be used for stories; they can also be super-effective for extension or cross-curricular activities. My favourite thing to do in my tents is UV work, which is amazingly successful. Cheap UV flashlights transform the tent into an underwater wonderland, an outer space adventure, a spooky cavern or a night-time escapade. Visual tracking, hand-eye coordination and comprehension all get a boost during UV sessions, and the items you discover can be the results of great mark-making or sensory craft lessons.

It is important to remember that your blackout tent is a super-special and exciting space to be in! Remind learners how lucky they are to step into this magical realm as you guide them through sensory wonders. In every classroom, blackout tents ignite imaginations, soothe senses and provide intimate spaces for engagement. So, here's to these extraordinary little dens – may they continue to spark joy and curiosity!

The Blackout Tent Cinema

Christy Townson, SEN teacher, Hillside Specialist School and College

We use a blackout tent as a small cinema, using the class iPads as screens. We read a social story in the tent to prepare students for a cinema trip, as some of them have never been to the cinema before.

For **Fatemah**, a SEN teacher at **Fairfield School**, blackout tents are a versatile piece of equipment for helping students enhance their focus, affording opportunities to engage more fully in their learning and the task at hand, and reducing anxiety by providing a space to regulate from noise and sensory overload.

Blackout Tents in the Classroom

Fatemah, SEN teacher, Fairfield School

I use blackout tents for sensory interventions in which students can explore different lights. To ensure that, as educators, we do our best for students to progress, we also make these cause-and-effect tents, in which students can press a switch to make the lights work. Our SEN students have MOVE targets. Students make the smallest of fine motor movements, which are celebrated as a big achievement, because by pressing the switch the lights come on. Especially for our PMLD students, a target like this is essential.

The uses of a blackout tent in class will depend on the needs of the students. Most classes will use theirs to ensure students get the best experience from their learning. The tent can be adapted to meet the needs of the whole class or individual students. The tent is usually not timetabled; it is brought for all classes that require it.

Sensory stories are used widely across the school. The needs of the students vary significantly, so I feel that sensory stories are best to accommodate all needs, as we can include something for every age and ability.

We accessorise our tents with props to deliver sensory stories and make them engaging.

The students really enjoy *We're Going on a Bear Hunt*, written by Michael Rosen. We have a 'cave' at the end and a little light for the bear's eyes, which is attached to a switch for the children to turn on.

Another good story we use a dark tent for is *Night Monkey and Day Monkey* by Julia Donaldson. For that part of the story set during the night time, we use the tent to sit in or, for big classes, a gazebo with all the sides down blocking the light, so everyone can fit in it comfortably. Then, when it is daytime in the story, everyone comes out of the tent.

Bothy Bags

These are used by hikers to provide protection from the elements when caught in bad weather or emergencies. Compact and lightweight, they are designed to be unfolded and quickly set up to create a small shelter, providing a temporary refuge to keep dry and warm until conditions improve.

Dome Tents

Dome tents have a rounded shape and offer more headroom than A-frame tents.

Fishing Shelters and Bivvies

These provide shelter from the elements. Their colour blends with nature, making them ideal for use in a forest school or outdoor environment as birdwatching or nature hides. Incorporate natural materials – bark, grass and non-toxic foliage, plants and flowers – to create a connection to the outdoors and a sensory haven.

Geodesic Domes

Geodesic domes create a microclimate. Plant exotic plants such as aloe vera, figs, lemon trees and bay trees; add seating and a portable solar fountain as a water feature.

Inflatable Tents

These are available in many different designs and sizes. Their beams become rigid when inflated with air and are easily deflated by squeezing. They are lightweight, compact and easy to store. They are fun to use and afford an opportunity to practise teamwork and perseverance as the group take turns to inflate the tent using a pump.

Pop-up Tents

Pop-up tents have a sprung design, enabling them to pop open in seconds and then fold flat for storage. They are easy to wipe clean and can be vacuumed or shaken outdoors. A cheap space-saving option for younger students, they can double up as a place for relaxation; be accessorised into an immersive learning space; or be used as a sensory retreat or pop-up dark room for vision impairment activities, which can be placed in the corner of a room if you do not have a permanent one in your setting.

Using Tents for Close-up Exploration

Louise Mills, teacher, London

I teach pupils at home, so my sensory tents need to be portable and easy to use. When sharing a sensory story inside a tent, depending on the learner, I lay the props out for free exploration after the story, supporting learners who do not access materials independently to explore each item. Some learners can see things close-up, so having the tent encloses the space, giving them better access to see things closer rather than the distraction of having objects around the room.

Tipis

Tipis are traditionally made from wooden poles arranged in a circle, then covered with animal hides or canvas. They have aesthetic appeal, can be used as a teaching tool to study Indigenous cultures and traditions, have more vertical space than a tent and are durable.

Tents and tipis are a way of bringing people together. Here, **Susie McClue**, senior connecting families development officer at **Scottish Families Affected by Alcohol and Drugs**, shares the story of her 'Kid's Tent', which she created during lockdown.

Kid's Tent

Susie McClue

I got a lot of joy bringing this together – it was a creative outlet during lockdown. I set this up in my garden in 2020 to promote an online festival that two colleagues and I organised for families.

The photo was used to promote the 'Kid's Tent', which involved four craft sessions in partnership with **Make Do Grow CIC** and two story sessions in partnership with **JustB**.

Our 'Connect, Communicate, Learn, and Thrive' Festival offered 11 different online activities for families and friends affected by a loved one's alcohol or drug use. It was an ideal opportunity for our community to stay connected and to meet people not currently known to us through our day-to-day work or services.

We reached people from 27 of the 32 council areas of Scotland, as well as in Northern Ireland, England and the USA. We received overwhelmingly positive feedback from those who participated:

> Everything has been perfect ... I didn't really know what to expect and the whole experience has surpassed my expectations. It has ticked all the boxes of your summer festival. I have connected with others in such a short space of time on a level that I would never imagined possible. I have learned to communicate in a way I never thought I was capable.
>
> – Festival attendee

> Encouraging and so good to be with other folk going through similar things. Really good ideas to help with stress, self-care, communication ...
>
> – – Festival attendee

This feedback has inspired us to keep developing our offering of online events and activities.

FIGURE T.2 Kid's Tent.
Photograph by Susie McClue

Tunnel Tents

Tunnel tents have a long, narrow shape and curved design that maximise interior space. They are wider at the centre and taper at the ends, providing stability in windy conditions. Their multiple entrances and vestibules provide convenient access to the tent and extra storage space for teaching resources. Combining physical activity with sensory stimulation, the tunnel supports the development of motor skills and is a space for exploration.

Jill Goodwin is an artist and researcher with an interest in sensory theatre. She was previously a teacher for children with profound intellectual and multiple disabilities. As part of her doctoral research, in which she explored the conditions that might enhance 'in the moment' presence for staff alongside pupils within a school for children with PMLD, Jill created Golden Tent: a large satin-covered structure with a reflective golden floor. Golden Tent was also integral to 'Space for Peace', an interfaith choral promenade event held in 2017 and 2018, and formed part of the sensory theatre training module for actor musician students at Rose Bruford College in 2023.

Golden Tent

Jill Goodwin

Golden Tent is a large (9m x 4.5m x 2.3m), cocoon-like enclosure with yellow satin walls and a reflective golden floor. It is an immersive space for 'being' rather than 'doing', created as part of a PhD study and erected in the hall of a school for children with profound intellectual and multiple disabilities. The sensorial conditions inside the tent are designed to promote stillness and to encourage busy classroom staff to shift from 'doing' to 'being' mode in order to be more 'present in the moment' alongside their pupil partners.

Feedback from staff who took part in the study suggested that being inside Golden Tent heightened awareness, enabling them to notice subtle expressions and behaviour from pupils that they might have missed in a busy classroom environment. Some felt that the language-free time enabled learners to come more to the fore.

> You don't think about what's got to be done next; you're completely in the moment.
>
> It's really relaxing – a space for being watchful as well as responding.
>
> It's a little moment of, 'What do you want to do …?'

In this way, Golden Tent can be seen as a space that enables staff to temporarily relinquish language (and learning targets) in order to be with pupils in a different way. It supports stillness and presence so that staff can hold the space for learners to come to the fore.

FIGURE T.3 Golden Tent.
Photograph by Jill Goodwin

Imagining Autism Pods

Imagining Autism (iA) was initiated as a collaboration between the disciplines of drama and psychology that sought to address the differences in communication, social interaction and imagination in autistic children. Funded by the Arts and Humanities Research Council (2011-2014) and based at the University of Kent, iA worked with the School of Arts, the Tizard Centre, the School of Psychology and the Gulbenkian Theatre. The project has since expanded into researching and celebrating autistic creativity and imagination as a source of wellbeing and learning, and establishing a substantial public engagement programme.

An iA pod is a tented structure with lights and sound performance co-produced with young people with sensory play opportunities within.

Kath Hart, a SEN teacher at the **Beacon School**, Folkestone, uses iA pods in a variety of ways with her Year 3 autistic children.

iA Pods

Kath Hart

I have a tent that I use to access different themes and topics to enhance the learning and focus of the children. I also have a tent I use for storytime with cushions, soft toys and blankets so the children can get comfy while listening to a story.

I have used tents in a variety of ways when using iA, which is a great way to engage autistic children through hands-on experiences, retelling, props and participation. A few teachers have iA pods in their classrooms which they theme towards the learning each term. It is a great way to encourage learning. We were a pilot school with the university to develop iA.

Creating a story-themed iA pod is an exciting way to immerse the story explorer and promote literacy skills as they become the author of their own stories by exploring the props.

For example, for 'The Three Little Pigs', suggested props/accessories might include the following:

- The straw house: Straw/dried grass/hay/shredded wheat/shredded paper.
- The wooden house: Twigs/sticks/cinnamon sticks/wooden craft sticks.
- The brick house: LEGO/DUPLO/Stickle Bricks/wooden blocks.

- 'I'll huff and I'll puff': Incorporate activities to practise blowing and strengthen mouth motor skills using bubbles, drinking straws, feathers, kazoos, party blowers, tissue paper and windmills. Other items to recreate the wolf's breath blowing include balloons, a battery-operated/manual/paper/card fan or a bicycle pump/bellows/foot pump.
- Add sound effects played via an app or recorded onto a sound button: a pig squealing, a wolf howling, the wind blowing, knocking on a door, building site sounds, sticks snapping.
- Recreate the sound of knocking on a door using a block and beater.
- Stick straw onto newspaper and drape over your tent to create an authentic straw house.

Deputy principal **Joe White** and assistant principal **Caroline Jaques** of **Meadowfield School** in Kent explain how iA pods enrich learning experiences.

Enhancing Educational Experiences using iA Pods

Joe White and Caroline Jaques

Our aim at Meadowfield is to create an immersive, captivating experience for our children to experience on a weekly basis. This is linked to a termly topic and accessed during early aid and communication sessions. Our intention is to have a positive impact on the children's imagination skills, which can then be transferred into the classroom.

Past topics include 'Jack and the Beanstalk', The Three Bears' and 'Little Red Riding Hood'. The students noticed the giant in the clouds, roleplayed building houses for the pigs and dressed up as the wolf.

The children have enjoyed exploring being under the sea. We have had a sea projector, wave crashing music, a bubble machine, sea animals, sand and water. The children have pretended to swim, built sandcastles and roleplayed pirates. We have also found treasure the pirates left!

CASE STUDY: IA POD

- Imagination Level December 2022 (Term 2) – 16-26B.
- Imagination Level March 2023 (Term 4) – 16-26E+.
- A case study of a pupil in Ducklings (EYFS).

Prior to using the iA pod, Pupil A found it difficult to play. He would line up objects repeatedly. Pupil A then began to access the iA pod at the beginning of term 3.

After weekly sessions, Pupil A's imaginative play skills began to develop and in the space of two terms, it had moved up five levels. He now demonstrates this play in the classroom and is beginning to roleplay with a small world set-up.

FIGURE T.4 The 'Three Little Pigs' themed iA pod.
Photograph by Meadowfield EYFS Team

Novelty Tents

There are many repurposed household items and unusual materials that you can use to construct a unique and exciting space for people to enjoy.

I delivered a lesson on Cleopatra when exploring the topic of Egypt. I made a boat using cardboard boxes painted gold and attached a purple-coloured fabric 'sail', lightly spritzed with perfume to recreate how Cleopatra coated the sails of her boat in fragrance that wafted to shore to let everyone know she was on her way.

If you have a budget, you can buy novelty tents shaped like animals, camper vans, sliced watermelon, sandwiches – even a tent shaped like a train going into a tunnel in the London Underground!

Claire Graham, activity coordinator and founder of **Inclusion Un.Limited**, created a tent using inflatable swimming rings.

Inflatable Swimming Ring Tent

Claire Graham

We were inspired by the artwork 'Summer Igloo' by Virginia Melnyk. We wanted to create a fun and eye-catching large tent space for a local outside event. It was an investment piece, as we had to purchase over 20 swimming hoops and multiple cable ties.

We experimented with different shapes for our large tent. Using PVC piping, we created a pyramid shape, which was more stable in the wind; however, it had a pipe at the entrance which would have made it difficult for hoist entry. We explored using a gazebo and attaching a wall of swimming hoops, which was easy to construct and stable.

We really enjoyed building the sensory igloo shape to replicate Virginia Melnyk's work; however, as this was only for a single-day event, we felt it was a waste of plastic. It was a fabulous sensory space once created: the small space felt spacious due to the air flow through the holes. The translucent colours were visually stimulating, and when outside, multiple shadows were created from the tent.

FIGURE T.5 Summer Igloo.
Photograph by Claire Graham

FIGURE T.6 Claire in her Summer Igloo.
Photograph by Claire Graham

Sophie Davey, SEN early years lead at **Manor Green Primary School**, West Sussex, was inspired by Claire's inflatable swimming ring tent and recreated this to make a hoop for their Home Corner.

Hula Hoop Home Corner

Sophie Davey

This was our EYFS colour topic. We had a large group of complex learners in the cohort, so we focused on exploring colour through our senses and in the natural light. This allowed for natural exploration of shadows, reflections and shapes. The hoops were cable tied to our metal water wall.

FIGURE T.7 Hula Hoop Home Corner.
Photograph by Sophie Davey

Retreat Tent

A sensory retreat provides a person with a quiet and private space to take a step out of current surroundings, nurturing physical, mental and emotional wellbeing, and enabling them to decompress and regroup if overstimulated. Offering a retreat space promotes independence as individuals learn to recognise their emotions and self-regulate.

In some settings, a retreat tent may be referred to as a 'safe space' for a person to access for privacy when feeling anxious, angry or upset. This can be part of a person's behaviour management plan.

A retreat tent should never be used as a form of isolation or a form of discipline.

Setting up a Retreat Zone

Locate it in a quiet, private space within view of adults. Ask whether the person would like an adult nearby for conversation, hand massage, guidance through yoga poses or breathing exercises, or simply for silent company. Some individuals may prefer to be alone.

Accessorise the retreat to meet the needs of the individual:

- Cushions, blankets, throws, beanbags, weighted blankets, neck wraps, body wraps and teddies provide comfort.
- A baseball cap, eye mask, sunglasses and ear defenders dull sound and light if the person is experiencing sensory overload.
- A poster or feelings board can help people identify and reflect on their feelings.
- Hang instructional posters with breathing exercises or yoga poses.
- Drawing and colouring are therapeutic, helping to calm the nervous system. Providing pencils, materials, books and worksheets can be helpful. Additionally, items such as playdough, fidget spinners and other tactile objects to push, pull, squeeze and manipulate are excellent additions to your calm space.
- Provide music and headphones.
- Massage lowers stress and anxiety and aids relaxation. Place a basket of massage tools and creams (unscented and scented) for the person to use independently or offer to help.
- A microwaveable wheat bag provides warmth (when heated in a microwave) and cold (when placed in the freezer). Both hot and cold temperatures can be soothing.
- Include a timer in the tent.
- For some people, less is more, so you may wish to have a decluttered space with just a blanket, throw, beanbag or cushion.

Taking deep, slow breaths helps people to calm down, but is often difficult to do when stressed or upset. **AnnMarie Walker** – who spent 25 years as both an SEN teacher and senior leader before taking her skills in a different direction by becoming a psychotherapist – recommends having a box of resources handy that promote deep breathing to use when a child is becoming anxious or dysregulated. In this box, you might include things such as:

- feathers to blow;
- bubbles;
- blow football-type activities; and
- pinwheels/windmills.

These are all quick activities that can engage children in deep breathing, which will slow down their heart rate, lower blood pressure and reduce muscle tension and anxiety.

AnnMarie explains that breathing and grounding exercises can help redirect negative or anxious thoughts and feelings through engaging the senses in the here and now.

One example is the '5, 4, 3, 2, 1' senses technique. In this, you ask the person to:

- name five things they can see;
- name four things they can touch;
- name three things they can hear;
- name two things they can smell; and
- name one thing they can taste.

Tigger Pritchard is a hybrid keynote speaker and conference presenter who offers training and consultancy to support individuals who are neurodivergent and their families. Tigger describes himself as 'awesomely neurodivergent and extremely passionate about enabling all to be more neuroinclusive, more neuroaffirming'.

Here, Tigger shares his experiences of using a tent to reduce his anxiety.

Retreat Tent for Adults

Tigger Pritchard

I have often used a tent to reduce my anxiety. I have a bright yellow Terra Nova Quasar (I also used to be a Duke of Edinburgh Award leader for many years).

I even put the tent up in my living room once and just stayed inside reading books and listening to the radio. I found it immensely peaceful! When I realised I was autistic all those years later, I completely understood why!

I found that the colour of the tent would have an impact on individuals – for example, a blackout tent would be better for some; while for others, colours or patterns would be impactful.

Often, which one I used would depend on the individual, but also on their anxiety levels at that time. So, I very much used the colour to impact on the experience, sometimes using additional lights to create the visual landscape inside.

Shower Tents

Shower tents are enclosed structures designed for taking outdoor showers, often when camping. They are constructed from lightweight, waterproof or water-resistant materials that fold away into compact bags, with a removable floor which enables them to slip easily over a wheelchair. They are easy to set up and take down.

Shower tents can also be repurposed to make sensory spaces. Combine a shower tent with a solar camping shower bag with a hose and showerhead, then step into a rainy day for a weather theme.

Abi Nicholls is a SEN teaching assistant from Cambridgeshire with an interest in supporting individuals with sensory processing disorders and autism. Abi shares her idea for an 'Under the Sea' tent.

Under the Sea Tent

Abi Nicholls

We created an 'Under the Sea' story tent using a light placed facing into the tent and battery lights threaded around the tent frame. We made tiny holes in the tent fabric, threaded wool through and hung fish shapes cut out from shiny card, so the fish were double-sided. We ripped up green tissue paper for seaweed and placed this on the floor of the tent and decorated the outside of the tent with pebbles and shells.

The students interacted as part of a theme for a sensory-based session as an opportunity to use various senses and experiences. They were involved in the design and implementation of the piece and explored it as the tent came to life.

The learning outcome was increased awareness of the environment as part of a recycling theme.

UV Tents

UV sensory exploration is an engaging way to promote focus, visual tracking and hand-eye coordination. These spaces can be created in any dark space – for example, a pop-up tent, a blackout tent or a space built using materials. Accessorise using glow-in-the-dark and fluorescent objects and toys: balls, beanbags, dice, putty, Flexitubes, gloves, mats, moon and stars, shakers and Slinkys. Explore UV paint and UV torches.

Richard Hirstwood, director of **Hirstwood Training**, describes UV torches as powerful sensory tools that enhance visual experiences by illuminating fluorescent objects, creating striking contrasts that capture attention. Here, Richard shares his top tips for using UV torches.

Top Tips for Using UV Torches

Richard Hirstwood

- Shine the UV torch on fluorescent objects to encourage visual tracking and engagement.
- Use the UV light to reveal hidden drawings or messages made with UV-reactive pens.
- Create a sensory scavenger hunt by illuminating various fluorescent items in a dark room.
- Explore different textures by highlighting fluorescent sensory materials such as body scrubs or ribbons.
- Enhance storytime by using the UV torch to make specific elements in UV-reactive story props glow.

Samantha, a former primary school teacher, is the owner of **Poppet Tops** and runs baby and toddler classes for fun, bonding and development. Samantha filled a tent with 3D shapes, clear ball pit balls, an infinity mirror, light cubes and a fibreoptic lamp to invite curiosity.

UV Safety Guidance

- Always supervise all activities and interactions with UV resources.
- Ensure items are not mouthed or chewed.
- Some of the items on the list may contain batteries. Ensure they are secured and not leaking.
- Discontinue use of UV items if they show signs of wear, tear or damage.
- Follow your setting's guidance as to time spent exposed to UV light.
- Your setting may have policies around people with epilepsy, require you to wear glasses or limit exposure to 30-minute sessions.

T Trampolines

Many special schools have trampolines and incorporate rebound therapy into their timetable. They offer therapeutic and physical benefits, aid posture and can be used to facilitate sensory experiences. **Elaine Burgess** is a senior teaching assistant and rebound therapy lead at **St Giles' School**. With a passion for supporting learners' physical, emotional and sensory development, Elaine has extensive experience in implementing rebound therapy to help students achieve their full potential. In her role, Elaine leads the integration of therapeutic practices to enhance student engagement and wellbeing, fostering a supportive and enriching learning environment.

Elaine and her colleague deliver weekly sessions incorporating sensory items into their sessions, as Elaine explains here.

Incorporating Sensory Tools into Rebound Therapy

Elaine Burgess

Rebound therapy is a therapeutic approach that utilises a trampoline to enhance physical, emotional and sensory development. In addition to the trampoline, we incorporate various sensory tools, such as sensory umbrellas, foil blankets, textured parachutes and hoops with lights, which are integrated into rebound therapy to further enrich the experience for our learners. Working within schools, we link the activities to the various topics learners are exploring in their classes. Additionally, we incorporate music alongside these tools to enhance engagement and create a multisensory experience. These tools engage our learners on multiple sensory levels, creating a more holistic and enriching therapeutic environment.

Sensory Umbrellas

Sensory umbrellas are creative and interactive tools in rebound therapy, designed with vibrant colours, lights and textures to stimulate a learner's visual and tactile senses. The umbrella can be moved gently over a learner as they bounce or jump, creating a sense of anticipation and excitement. It can also provide a shaded space, offering learners a break from bright lights and intense stimuli, creating a calming effect.

FIGURE T.8 Sensory equipment used during rebound therapy sessions. Photograph by Elaine Burgess

Foil Blankets

These are lightweight and designed to reflect body heat. In rebound therapy, they provide a valuable sensory experience. Their crinkly sound and shiny, reflective surface offer both auditory and tactile input, which is highly beneficial for our learners. A learner can be wrapped in a foil blanket to provide a calming effect through deep pressure stimulation. This can help regulate sensory processing and reduce feelings of overstimulation or anxiety that may arise after intense physical activity.

Textured Parachutes

These are an excellent tool for engaging learners in rebound therapy. When bouncing our learners on the trampoline, we may use the parachute above them. This provides an opportunity for them to feel the varying textures and materials hanging from the parachute and experience a sense of movement or resistance as the fabric moves up and down. The parachute's swaying motion offers vestibular stimulation, helping our learners regulate their spatial awareness.

The parachute can also be attached to a wire that hangs over the mat. Learners can move towards it, exploring the different textures and grasping the various ribbons, bells etc that are attached. This is especially beneficial for learners with sensory integration needs, as it can also serve as a comforting tool. Being enveloped in the soft fabric of the parachute can have a grounding effect, helping to soothe learners who may experience heightened anxiety or overstimulation.

The tactile experience of feeling different textures on the body, combined with the physical movement of the trampoline, can assist in building body awareness and developing sensory processing skills.

Hoops with Lights and Materials

These can add an exciting visual dimension to rebound therapy. For example, we use LED lights that can change colours or patterns, creating a dynamic and engaging visual experience. When learners are bouncing, we use the hoops around them to guide their movement on the trampoline bed, and they can hold onto the hoops and explore the textures. Learners who are lying on mats or wedges can explore the hoops with us, using hand-under-hand support, hand-over-hand support and physical and verbal prompting.

The lights can help learners track movements and enhance their focus. The rhythmic changes in light patterns can also have a calming or energising effect, depending on the design, encouraging learners to adapt to the changing environment.

By using these sensory tools creatively, you can foster a supportive, engaging and therapeutic environment that promotes learning, self-expression and physical development.

Emma Pauley is an artist, designer, researcher, public speaker, campaigner and award-winning entrepreneur who, through her business, People as Partners, is dedicated to ensuring that disabled people and carers are supported to live a good life. Emma's youngest daughter, Millie, was born with a very rare genetic condition called TUBA1a. Here Emma shares her ideas for weaving sensory experiences into daily routines.

Ball Pit Balls and Trampoline Tent

Emma Pauley and Millie

Using plastic ball pit balls on the trampoline is so much fun. Bouncing and watching them go up and down with each jump gives Millie so much joy. This activity has been good for learning colours and counting, as well as practising throwing skills. We have a trampoline tent. The girls love to take cushions and blankets into the tent. It's a great hideaway, perfect for relaxing after their jumping sessions.

T Trellises

Used to support plants as they grow, add height and create a vertical garden, trellises can be used indoors and outdoors.

Hook small pots onto the trellis, place growbags at the base and plant herbs, strawberry plants, pick-and-eat salads and peas to promote sustainable living.

Growbags are self-contained gardens and can be placed on a table for accessibility while planting. Arrange plants by theme (eg, basil, cherry tomatoes, chillies, onions, oregano and thyme for a pizza topping theme) or colour (eg, yellow edible flowers such as dandelions, marigolds, nasturtiums and squash blossoms); plant mixed herbs or sow wildflowers to attract bees and butterflies.

In a classroom setting, attach a trellis to a wall and use laundry pegs to display artworks and crafts, showcasing student creativity. For a themed sensory area, enhance the learning environment by placing a trellis between two desks facing each other, acting as both a divider and an interactive space. A trellis can also be secured flat against the ceiling as a space for hanging sensory items.

T Tunnels

Children are curious and often make tunnels using bedsheets, blankets and existing furniture. You can purchase buy pop-up concertina tunnels or Lycra tunnels; make a tunnel by taping cardboard boxes together; or lay a piece of fabric on the floor for children to crawl under.

Crawling through tunnels develops somatosensory perception (body awareness). In PE lessons, incorporate different sensory experiences into tunnels. Drape thick, black fabric over one end of a tunnel to create darkness and offer a headtorch to aid navigation. In another tunnel, place feathers, sponges, ball pit balls and scented items such as lavender sachets or citrus peel inside for the tunnel explorer(s) to find and collect. Line a tunnel with foil or bubble wrap to produce auditory feedback or link together to make one long tunnel. Attach a pop-up tent den at the end.

Place battery lights around the exit of the tunnel and incorporate the tunnel into a sensory story involving a cave, tunnel or hideout. Add sound buttons in the tent to provide sound effects or play music through a speaker.

U Umbrellas

Sensory umbrellas are a portable tool to engage the senses. They can easily be accessorised to complement a theme or topic; or collaborate with the sensory explorer to create an umbrella using their favourite items, making it a personalised sensory experience.

To accessorise an umbrella, add texture by wrapping sensory items such as ribbon, tinsel or bubble wrap around the handle. Incorporate sound by clipping a Talking Peg or other sound-producing objects to the ribs of the umbrella. Hang scented items, such as potpourri or dried lemon peel threaded onto string; or place a few drops of essential oil onto the fabric of the umbrella panels. Decorating the fabric panels of the umbrella with seasonal elements (eg, leaves for an autumn theme) or projecting lights or images adds a visual interest.

Explore different types of umbrellas:

- **Beach umbrellas** are large, making them perfect for providing ample shade. Many come with UV protection to help shield against the sun's rays. Their sturdy base makes them portable and convenient for use in any setting.
- **Bubble umbrellas** are domed-shaped and smaller and are thus easier for younger children to hold and handle. They can also be used to create a smaller sensory space.
- **Colour-changing** umbrellas have special inks on their panels that react to water, temperature and UV light.
- **Golf umbrellas** are large and sturdy, providing more coverage than a standard umbrella – ideal for sharing space with another person. Some feature a pointed end which enables them to be anchored into the ground, providing additional stability when used outdoors.
- **Novelty umbrellas** are available in many fun designs, including inside-out umbrellas and umbrellas with flashing lights. Umbrellas shaped like characters or animals can serve as a base for creating a sensory story – for example, tie feathers, lily pad leaves, toy dragonflies, fish, plastic ducks, frogs, foliage, a bunch of fresh grass or sparkly blue or green fabric to represent water ripples onto a frog-shaped umbrella to create an engaging and imaginative story about a pond.
- **Rainbow-coloured umbrellas** are fun to use in storytelling (eg, David McKee's Elmer books, *The Colour Monster* by Anna Llenas and *The Wizard of Oz* by L Frank Baum).
- **Umbrella hats** are hands-free and can be adapted using props.
- **Transparent umbrellas** let in natural light and offer a clear view, enabling people to maintain visual contact with their surroundings and with others.

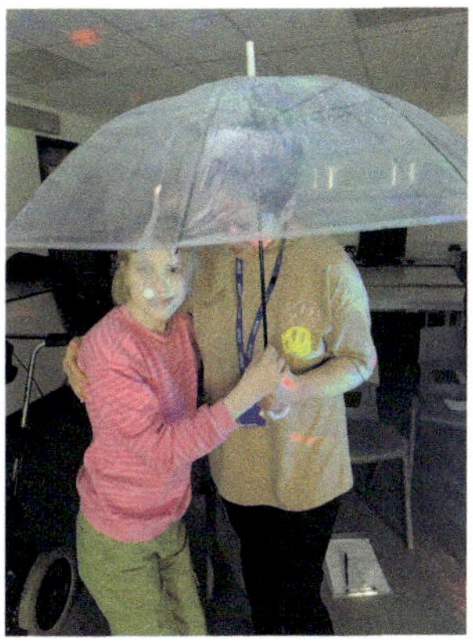

FIGURE U.1 Sophie and student under the Festival Umbrella. Photograph by Julia Barnes

Teacher **Julia Barnes** from **Ravenscliffe High School** shares a photo taken when her class was sharing a story about attending a music festival. The learner was dancing when rain was threatened in the story. A transparent umbrella was offered which she hid under with the staff member supporting her, and they sheltered from the water-spray rain.

Louise Mills, a teacher from London, teaches pupils at home and uses clear umbrellas as an effective part of her sensory stories.

Transparent Umbrellas

Louise Mills

I theme my sensory umbrellas – it's easier for me to tell and be more passionate about a nature-based theme or a sensory story from a book, story or poem, or one I have written.

Having a story focus helps the experience to flow better and using the umbrella gives children the opportunity to see things around that story underneath the umbrella. If I were telling a story about winter, I would have all the objects blue, white and sparkly and incorporate smells such as peppermint. I use clear string to hang the items, as it is discreet and unobtrusive.

The clear umbrellas create the feeling of being enclosed, but students can look around and see things from a different perspective and learn how to focus on the object or objects closest to them.

FIGURE U.2 Building the anticipation.
Photograph by Victoria Navin

I delivered a multisensory story workshop at **Hebden Green School** in Winsford, Cheshire. The teams worked in groups. They were given the text to a sensory story and had 15 minutes to source props from their classrooms; they then returned to work on their stories before sharing them with the other groups.

One group delivered a story on 'The Weather'. For the line, 'I like to play out in the rain, splashing in puddles that swirl down the drain,' they used a clear umbrella as a shield against the 'rain', which was sprinkled onto the umbrella using a watering can. This is ideal for students who do not like the sensory feedback of water, as they can experience the sound and sight of the 'rain' without getting wet and can see what is happening through the transparent umbrella.

Amy Wells of **Riverside School** incorporates sensory umbrellas into 'circle time', creating a soothing environment to calm students during a busy period when they are transitioning into school.

Circle Time Umbrella

Amy Wells

We created an emotions umbrella which is used during our circle time to develop knowledge of emotions. We play a song relating to *The Colour Monster* story about emotions being associated with different colours, such as pink for love. We sing along as we twirl the umbrella around to the tempo of the music. The pupils track the material using their eyes, watching it swirl around them, smiling as it passes their faces. Sometimes they reach out for the material with their hands.

We chose to learn about emotions in circle time as it's important to support pupils in understanding their own emotions and how to regulate them. Learning emotions through colour is a great starting point for SEN pupils, who may learn in alternative ways.

Our umbrella provides a sensory and engaging way to learn about their emotions along with the music.

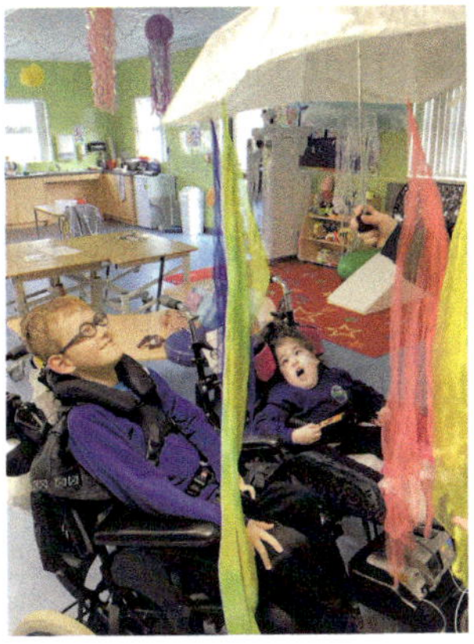

FIGURE U.3 Circle time umbrella.
Photograph by Amy Wells

If you are working in a school, a care home or a similar setting, making sensory umbrellas is a fun and educational hands-on activity.

Making SENse Creative, founded by **Caroline Hill**, offers multisensory opportunities for individuals to explore and celebrate their creativity and mark-making with a focus on the journey or process. Sensory artists are inspired to communicate imaginatively with exciting, unique, creative possibilities.

Caroline was invited to join the expert panel and present at the Story Massage Programme Conference held in May 2019 at the Arc Centre in London, where she delivered a sensory umbrella workshop.

Sensory Umbrella Workshop

Caroline Hill

I wanted this activity to be practical and hands-on, so I purchased 20 clear umbrellas and chose a couple of themes to look at, to involve a story massage and also make an object of reference. I wanted something that would be very sensory in terms of the learners we were supporting, so I came up with umbrellas because they are fun, simple objects and such a lovely way to make a personal and portable space.

The people attending the workshop were all given an umbrella. Working in pairs and threes, and using items I had brought in from home – cheap, everyday household objects such as sponges, carrier bags and bubble wrap to cut up – they created their umbrellas.

We showcased our umbrellas and then had a celebration, sitting singing underneath them, at the end of the workshop.

Tomoyo Nozaki, a complementary therapist from Japan, commented: 'The workshop was very enjoyable – it enhanced focus and encouraged kinetic mindfulness; and, with no goals or right answers, it naturally nurtured creativity.'

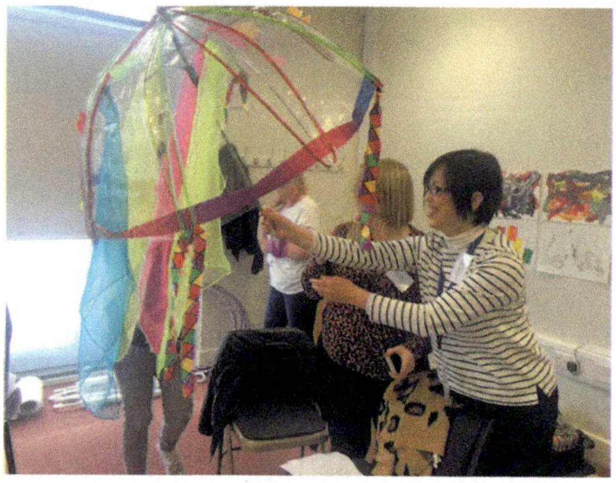

FIGURE U.4 Tomoyo Nozaki with a sensory umbrella.
Photograph by Caroline Hill

FIGURE U.5 Sensory umbrella workshop.
Photograph by Caroline Hill

Top Tips for Creating Sensory Umbrellas

- Mike Ayres projection umbrellas have safe ends, are available in black and white, and can be used with a portable projector or iPhone.
- Use sensory umbrellas alongside music. I created a seaside umbrella sensory experience using brightly coloured, stripey material and coloured chewy rock, playing the song 'I Do Like to be Beside the Seaside' by John H Glover-Kind.
- Theme your umbrellas – for example, 'Valentine's Day Hearts' or 'Under the Sea'.
- To create an underwater theme, light up the umbrella using battery LED fairy lights. Use parcel ties to secure the lights to the arms of the umbrellas. Add scents: Inis, Lush and Avon are some companies whose products have fresh seaside fragrances. Explore seaweed products; taste seaweed crackers. Work with different textures – objects that dangle down to brush the face and cheek, feathers and tinsel. Add items that make sounds; string shells together.
- You can use the simplest of items to make your umbrella. One example is colourful shower scrunchies.

Sensory umbrellas can be decorated using a variety of craft items to create a theme. **Sophie Davey**, SEN early years lead at **Manor Green Primary School** in West Sussex, shares her inspiring ideas here.

Themed Sensory Umbrellas

Sophie Davey

I love a sensory umbrella and thoroughly enjoy making themed umbrellas for my sensory engagement learners. As the early years lead in a special school, my background is with children with complex and severe learning difficulties, so anything sensory is very much up my street. I was thinking about how I could expand into using tents to create more stable sensory environments similar to my umbrellas. The bottom could be cut out and placed over someone, with lots of lovely hanging sensory items inside.

Another interesting idea is using a white tent to project onto, to create a sensory environment that is easily changeable.

The work featured in the photographs is my own creation, but as a school we are very creative – which is why I've been able to be so creative in my approach too. Thank you to all of the wonderfully creative teachers and support staff at Manor Green Primary.

The neon deep-sea UV glow umbrella created a neon sensory experience. Neon jellyfish, CDs and ribbons hung from the ribs of the umbrella. It was made for our 'The Little Mermaid' Christmas show for a learner with cerebral visual impairment, for whom the contrast was easier to manage. I needed to create a visually safe space for him to take away the overwhelming background, as there was an audience and there were lots of lights on. The umbrella clipped onto the back of his chair so that his mum and dad could see him, but he still had that safe space to allow him to be within the environment and engage.

We ensure all of our children have the opportunity to take part in our Christmas productions. Rather than them having to put on a show, we create these visually sensory experiences for them. Their families can then watch the live experiences during this sensory moment. That's where the umbrellas, hoop and leaves come in, because we want to showcase our children's engagement and show their families how much they love that.

FIGURE U.6 Deep-sea UV glow umbrella in daylight.
Photograph by Sophie Davey

FIGURE U.7 Deep-sea UV glow umbrella in the dark.
Photograph by Sophie Davey

Umbrellas can be divided into panels. I made an 'Autumn Dream' umbrella, with each panel telling a different part of the story. Leaves on one panel represented walking through the autumn leaves; there was a panel of lights for thunder and lightning; and a third panel represented the wind, with a wind chime on it. At the end of the story, we went into a dream, so we turned the (dream) lights off and were underneath the night sky with the UV moon (lighting).

A bumblebee umbrella was created using crepe and tissue paper, scalloped with scissors, then spiralled and taped from the top of the umbrella to the bottom. Fairy lights were woven through the paper; and the underneath of the umbrella had black netting with bumblebees I made.

FIGURE U.8 Bumblebee sensory umbrella.
Photograph by Sophie Davey

FIGURE U.9 Tiny Little Fly Sensory Story Umbrella made from a sock and bubble wrap.
Photograph by Sophie Davey

Sensory Story Umbrellas

Sophie Davey also revealed how she has created sensory story umbrellas for her learners by cleverly combining a sensory umbrella with story props and a visual background. In this video (https://tinyurl.com/2ru6e39a), Sophie tells the story of *The Rainbow Fish* by Marcus Pfister against the backdrop of footage of a coral reef under the sea playing on an interactive whiteboard.

The fish are suspended from the arms of the umbrella. 'They spin as they swim,' Sophie narrates as she spins the umbrella. 'Some of Rainbow Fish's friends are good at splashing' – Sophie sprays water. 'Other friends are very good at blowing bubbles' – Sophie fires bubbles from a bubble gun. The story continues: 'Rainbow Fish noticed a glimmer in the water and saw the stars had come out' – Sophie turns on string battery lights attached underneath the umbrella and the shiny, coloured Rainbow Fish reflects in the light. 'Rainbow Fish invited friends to play. "It's too dark," they said. But Rainbow Fish knew as the stars came out, he could guide the fish as he lit the way' – Sophie turns on the torch.

This video was filmed during lockdown, when Sophie's school filmed stories to send out to children's families.

FIGURE U.10 Rainbow Fish sensory umbrella.
Photograph by Sophie Davey

FIGURE U.11 Summer flowers.

Photograph by Sophie Davey

FIGURE U.12 Cloud for Peter Pan made with a deconstructed umbrella, paper lanterns and cushion filler, illuminated with fairy lights.

Photograph by Sophie Davey

V Vision Impairment Sensory Spaces

Gwyn McCormack, a qualified teacher of vision impairments and director of award-winning international business **Positive Eye**, shares tips to make experiences accessible and vision friendly for all.

Vision

Gwyn McCormack

Vision is the major source for people to learn, understand and make sense of the world. However, the demands of a visually cluttered environment make this challenging.

Your Face

Your face is an important resource in engaging and socially interacting, responding and conveying emotions. Our faces are typically low contrast: our lips and eyes don't stand out, yet these are two of the main features we use to engage with people.

Tip: Add contrast to your face. Wear red or black-framed glasses (lens removed), red lipstick, a black moustache, a red nose, black false eyelashes, darker eyebrows or black eyeliner.

Your Body

Your body is an important resource. You move around when interacting with a child (sitting, kneeling, lying down). It creates the backdrop when you are showing a child a resource.

Tip: What you wear matters – always. Change your practice and wear black. Think, 'How can I make it easier to see and to access learning?' The approaches benefit all children's access – they are inclusive of all.

FIGURE V.1 A cluttered background and surface, and a person dressed in colours or patterns, create distinct barriers to access.

Photograph by Gwyn McCormack

FIGURE V.2 Wear black, long-sleeved clothing, an apron or tabard and black gloves, and use a high-contrast resource.

Photograph by Gwyn McCormack

The Surface

The surface you are working on with the child matters – be it the floor, a tray, a tabletop or a beanbag cushion.

Tips: Cover the tray, table with black matt Fablon, cover the bean bag or area with a large piece of black felt/cloth or a black duvet cover or sheet, and use large pegs to hold it in place. Cover your knees, or smaller areas, with squares of black cloth.

The Background and the Resources

These also matter. Invest in a black tent or explore a portable background (see 'Dröna Boxes and Ability Communication Boards' on page 66). Anyone can create a vision-friendly environment with a few low-cost resources.

Ask Yourself ...

- Have I made it easier to access the activity?
- Have I maximised the opportunity to access the activity?
- What action did I take?
- Is there anything I would do differently next time?
- What worked well? What didn't work so well?

Pauline Woodcock, a SEN teacher at **Fairfield School**, uses vision impairment tents with her students.

Vision Impairment Tents

Pauline Woodcock

I have a PMLD class and use tents a lot to make individual working zones. I purchased small photographic tents for less than £50 online. I use these to create individual working zones for my students. They minimise distraction from other students, so they can focus on what they are doing. I have used them to develop cause and effect skills and visual tracking skills and have seen students make excellent progress. I change what lighting is used depending on what skills the student is working on. Each tent is large enough to accommodate wedges so the student can be positioned according to their individual therapy plans.

The tents are also very calming and can help regulate unsettled young people by giving them space and time away from the usual learning environment.

FIGURE V.3 Vision impairment tents.
Photograph by Pauline Woodcock

W Walls

A wall or display board is a blank canvas to transform into an immersive sensory space. Divide into zones or theme the entire wall. Some walls are made of hard concrete, making it difficult to staple onto them. One solution is to stick corkboard or cork tiles, foam panels or acoustic tiles (using heavy-duty adhesive) or thick fabric (using batons) to the wall.

Add interactive elements by attaching a magnetic strip or applying magnetic paint and attaching magnets to sensory items to enable them to be moved around to change the display. Alternatively, use Velcro. Paint a section of the wall using chalkboard paint for use as a working wall. If using paper, add scent.

CASE STUDY: A COLLABORATIVE SENSORY RAINFOREST WALL

Aim

For students to create a collaborative sensory wall display representing the sights, smells, textures and sounds of the rainforest.

Background Information

Twice weekly, a mixed ability class of ten Year 5 SEN students explored our half-term rainforest topic. My sensory pathway group of five students accessed learning through a sensory story. They were very engaged with the props, so we decided to make a living sensory wall.

Project Planning

We started with a blank wall in the classroom, with the idea of it being a work in progress that would evolve as we collected, explored, crafted and placed the materials on our wall during timetabled daily fine motor skill sessions and twice-weekly topic sessions.

Materials and Resources

Wherever possible, we incorporated natural elements collected from outdoors and also used items from our fabric scraps and recycling materials store.

Design and Construction

Bark chippings, soil and dried leaves were glued onto the wall to create the rainforest floor. Tree trunks were cut from cork and moss was glued on. We made tactile animals: coloured, feathered parrots; fake chamois leather capybaras; a crocodile made from a fake crocodile skin patterned leather belt; a monitor lizard with sandpaper skin; and a 3D snake made using brown mesh packing paper we had stuffed with newspaper, rolled into a snake shape and painted. We made coffee bushes using leaves and twigs, glued on coffee beans and added ferns, grasses and potpourri.

We planted beans and peas into paper disposable cups during a science lesson, which were stapled onto the wall. Student A was allocated the job of misting the leaves and watering the plants.

We added sound hanging seed pods and recorded rainforest animal calls onto sound buttons, placing them next to the corresponding animals.

Student Involvement

All students contributed to the wall. We explored a variety of earthy and woody essential oils, choosing sandalwood oil to scent the trees, as it was important that everyone liked the smell we chose.

Challenges and Solutions

We were unsure of the longevity of our display. It was September term and Student B had moved up a year and joined the class. Student B found the sound and action of ripping paper soothing and it helped with his sensory regulation. He had historically ripped down classroom displays, so his previous classes had placed Perspex over their wall displays to prevent this, meaning the displays had no sensory feedback other than the flat, hard Perspex.

Student B was drawn to the sensory feedback of a piece of brown corduroy fabric and started ripping it, so was assigned the job of making the lianas (jungle vines).

Impact

Building the sensory rainforest provided opportunities for students to explore and express their likes, dislikes and sensory preferences through the handling of different sensory items and materials. They were engaged and settled into the daily sessions. They had opportunities to work on fine motor skills, creativity and self-expression; and the topic work connected them to biodiversity, biology, ecology, geography and nature.

Both staff and students found the wall created and enhanced a calm learning environment. Students from the semi-formal pathway group contributed to the rainforest wall too, making items during art lessons.

During snack time, we would smell, touch and sample tropical fruit: fresh, dried and juiced banana, guava, lychees, mango, papaya, pineapple, passion fruit and rambutan – and two brave students explored the stinky durian.

At the end of the seven-week term, the plants cascaded down the walls.

Conclusion

This was a fully inclusive activity whereby all students became the creators of their classroom surroundings, creating a sensory wall that offered a sensory-rich experience that also supported the curriculum topic. The students were proud of their wall and a little sad when it was dismantled at the end of term.

To sum up, sensory walls are an opportunity for students to personalise their learning space, which fosters a sense of ownership and pride and enhances learning.

To improve in the future, I would place suction cup holders on the wall and hang wedding favour bags filled with ginger root, turmeric powder, lemongrass sticks and perfume to represent the smells of the rainforest. I would link QR codes with footage of the rainforest and direct a projector with green light to illuminate the display when the lights are dimmed in the classroom.

We continued making our sensory wall displays, moving onto ancient Greece and making a giant mouth, complete with tongue and teeth, to support our healthy living topic.

W Washing Lines

Retractable washing lines can be used indoors. They are height adjustable, so can accommodate standing frame and wheelchair users, or a person lying on the floor. They can quickly be retracted to tidy away after an activity.

Peg on sensory items to make a sensory line: tie on cloth bags containing scented items or hang visually stimulating items onto the line.

Attach sock peg spinners to make sensory stations; group items (eg, textures) or invite the sensory space user to select their favourite items to place on the spinner.

Dry and display paintings; peg on activity cards, number/alphabet cards, a visual schedule or props from a story to sequence.

Drape a sheet or blanket over a heavy-duty washing line to make a tent, pulling the material outwards to form a tent shape, weighing down the sides using sandbags and making an opening using bulldog clips.

Secure to existing structures (eg, trees, a fence or railings) and hang pots, pans, plastic bottles filled with pebbles and sand, windchimes, PVC pipes and other items to make a sound line. Provide sticks and utensils to strike the items with to explore sound.

W Wigwams and Tipis

Conical in shape with a pointed top resembling the design of a Native American tipi, these canvas structures are strong and sturdy. You can buy indoor and outdoor tipis.

Make a living tipi by pushing garden canes into the ground in a semicircle, ensuring they are evenly spaced. Tie the tops of the canes together and place cane caps or plastic bottles on the end of the canes for safety. Plant fast-growing plants such as runner beans, nasturtiums or sweet peas around the base of each cane. This creates a natural hideaway which encourages outdoor play and a connection with nature, and teaches the value of patience and the rewards of nurturing living things.

You can buy a readymade runner bean wigwam and use this as your base.

Beccy Miller is a complementary therapy practitioner. During one of her sessions at **Tŷ Hafan Hospice** in South Wales, Beccy turned the lounge area into a camping experience for the children using a pop-up wigwam and sensory props. The children joined in the 'Camping Adventure' follow-along massage story shown on the screen, written, recorded and demonstrated by Mary Atkinson of the Story Massage Programme.

Camping Adventure

Beccy Miller

I chose the camping theme after seeing Mary Atkinson demonstrate this on her YouTube channel and thinking how wonderful it would be to adapt it for my place of work (Tŷ Hafan Children's Hospice).

Story massage is a great way to promote positive touch, enhancing calmness and creativity. I wanted to make the session as interactive as possible, to let the children experience not only the sensation of the massage strokes, but also the visual experience of the tent and campfire, and the smell and feel of the marshmallows.

My vision is always to make my Story massage sessions as inclusive as possible for all abilities of those who attend – whether they are a child with complex medical needs, a sibling, a parent or one of the care team. I hope everyone attending will get something from my session; but mainly I hope it's fun, and a fabulous sensory experience.

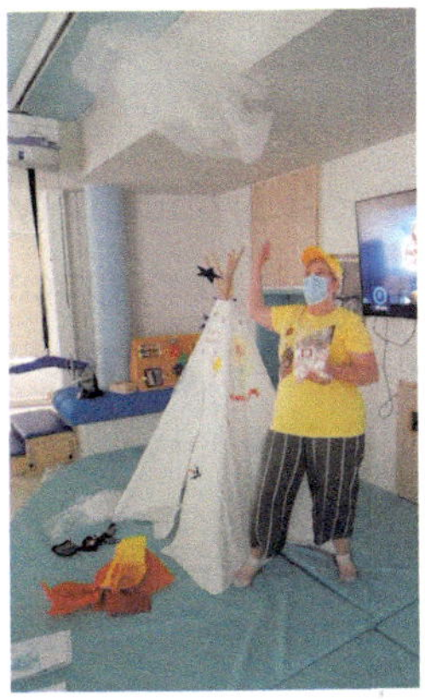

FIGURE W.1 Camping Adventure.
Photograph by Beccy Miller

Mary Atkinson is co-founder of the **Story Massage Programme** along with **Sandra Hooper**. They share a vision for championing the benefits of positive and respectful touch for children and adults of all ages and abilities.

The Story Massage Programme combines the benefits of nurturing touch with the fun and familiarity of storytelling. It presents opportunities for creativity and interaction, increasing engagement and communication. The story massage strokes are used to 'illustrate' the words of a story, poem or song, bringing them to life and making the activity fully inclusive for all learners. Further reported benefits include increased calmness and concentration, better relationships and improved social skills.

You can watch 'Camping Adventure' here: https://youtu.be/yw0rnfckGyE?si=vpVC6gjS01SQ5EPi

FIGURE W.2 Camping Adventure.
Photograph by Mary Atkinson

W Workspaces

Workspaces help maintain focus and boost productivity and learning. Many of the materials explored in the book can be used to create a workspace. Define the space using curtains, fabric ceiling hangings, furniture, plants, trellises, moveable wheeled dividers and rugs. For small activities, Dröna boxes can be placed on desks.

Create tech stations for interactive learning, use colour zones for various areas and accessorise with flexible seating (beanbags, chairs, standing desks or floor cushions).

Lynn McCann is a specialist teacher at **Reachout ASC**. Here she discusses the benefits of creating a private workspace.

The Benefits of Creating a Private Workspace

Lynn McCann

Both autistic and ADHD children are often easily distracted by the noise, movement and visual displays in the classroom; and, at home, by the noise, movement and goings-on of the rest of the family. There is real benefit in creating a private, cordoned-off space when they might be trying to do homework, need room to do a craft project or want to play with LEGO in peace.

A portable workspace or 'office' can provide everything the child needs in one place. A three-sided screen – either one you have bought or a plain cardboard box – makes the area private. It sends a clear 'do not disturb' signal to people nearby and allows the user to work somewhere free from visual distraction. Add a pair of headphones or loop ear-buds and they may be free from noise distractions too.

The benefit of portability is that after the task is finished, you can pack it all away and reclaim your dining table or bring the child back into the whole class lesson.

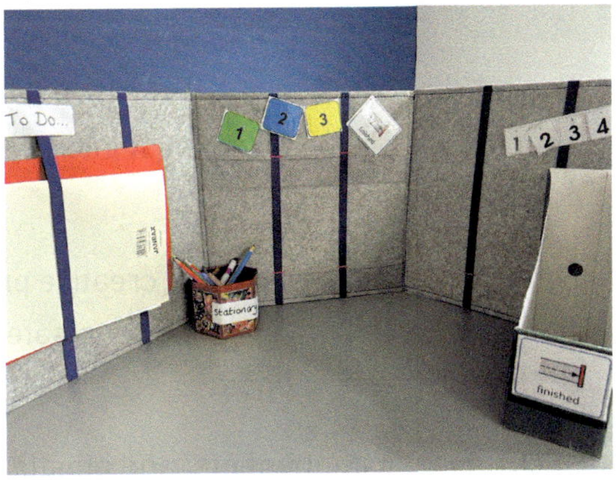

FIGURE W.3 Workspace screen.
Photograph by Lynn McCann

X Xylography

Xylography involves carving into a piece of wood, dipping it into ink and then pressing the wood onto paper to make a print.

A sensory xylography station invites learners to explore creative printmaking through a rich, multisensory experience. Balsa wood and foam sheets offer a safe, accessible surface for carving; corrugated cardboard has pre-scored lines.

Tools include blunt wooden sticks, plastic implements, and plastic modelling tools, making the activity accessible for all abilities. Tactile inking trays filled with thickened tempera or yoghurt-based paints – optionally infused with glitter, sand, or scents – and textured paper add instant tactile feedback.

Invite learners to press their designs using rolling pins, soft bricks, or gloved hands.

For a sensory-friendly twist, use clay, dough, plasticine or Playdoh.

Eighteen-year-old **Thor Kopperud** is Norwegian, with a Brazilian mother (Roberta), and lives in Rio de Janeiro. Thor's sensory space is his desk, where he makes beautiful sculptures. He loves Thomas the Tank Engine and wants to have an exhibition of his work in England, where the cartoon was produced. This year, Thor participated in three events about autism at **GALERIA AUT**, where he sold his works of art.

To make his sculptures, Thor uses tools (rolling pins, sticks and cutters) to shape, mould and cut 'Brazilian biscuit' – a modelling dough that dries with air contact. Thor shapes and colours his models using American paste (fondant) used to decorate cakes.

Sensory Sculptures

Thor and Roberta Kopperud

Thor: I feel inspired, calm, focused and happy when I'm modelling. I want to create new characters from the themes of cartoons and films (eg, Disney car collection, Ice Age, Pokémon).

Roberta: Thor reproduces both what he watched and liked, such as favourite cartoon characters, using Internet searches, and what he creates based on what he imagines.

FIGURE Z.1 Thor creating a sculpture.
Photograph by Roberta Kopperud

FIGURE Z.2 Thor's sculptures.
Photograph by Roberta Kopperud

Y Yoga Mat

A yoga mat can become a wonderfully adaptable sensory space, acting as a defined personal zone—something many learners find reassuring and grounding.

You can use a yoga mat as a calming space for mindful breathing, massage, meditation or simply lying still with dim lights and calming music.

Add sensory elements, such as bubble wrap, cork sheeting, cushions, faux fur and other fabrics, or foam tiles; create a tactile trail for fingers or feet. Mark the edges of the mat with ribbed or brightly coloured tape to help visually or physically define the space.

Recreate a sensory story on the mat using yoga poses. For example, for an animal theme, you could balance like a bird, curl into cat, extend into cobra, leap like a dolphin, stretch into downward dog, rise into eagle, lounge like a frog etc.

Z Ziploc® Sensory Bags

Cost-effective, simple to make and portable, a Ziploc sensory bag is a mess-free way for learners to safely engage in tactile exploration and experience colours and movement. Seal in items such as hair gel, oil, shaving foam, cooked pasta, water beads or dried beans and pulses for different textural sensations as learners squeeze them in their hands – the scope for their contents is limitless. Add colour, glitter or small objects. Theme a Ziploc bag – for example, for a Z-themed bag, you may wish to include a zebra toy, zebra-striped fabric, the zest of a citrus fruit, a zigzag pattern cutout or fabric and a zipper; or make a zoo-themed bag.

Next Steps

Now you have explored ideas on creating sensory structures, you can use and adapt them to create distinct zones/sensory spaces that provide different experiences catering to individual preferences, allowing people to explore and express their likes, dislikes and sensory preferences, and make rejections and choices. These can be linked to individual senses, activities or topics and themes.

A designated sensory space is ideal if you are working on an ongoing project or creating an immersive experience linked to a topic or theme you are currently exploring and do not wish to keep packing everything away at the end of the session – you can simply zip up your tent or gazebo. You may wish to change your themes weekly, fortnightly or termly.

The following part recaps the 'why', before the book concludes with some suggestions for creating your own sensory spaces/zones.

Part 4

THE 'WHY'

Sensory spaces/zones create a supportive and inclusive environment that enhances the physical, emotional and cognitive development of individuals. Whether they are young children, people with sensory processing needs, learning disabilities or adults with dementia, these spaces improve overall wellbeing and enrich lives.

Sensory spaces/zones can be set up in homes, nurseries, schools, colleges and daycare and residential care facilities. While the basic principles for setting up these spaces remain consistent, it is important to consider the purpose of the space and the reasons for creating it.

Sensory Zones in the Home

Purpose

By incorporating sensory spaces/zones in the home, parents, families and carers can create a supportive and nurturing environment that enhances the person's physical, emotional and cognitive development, contributing to their overall wellbeing and quality of life.

A sensory zone in the home can be tailored to meet the unique needs and preferences of the individual. It may be a dedicated room or a specific corner; or, as explored elsewhere in the book, centred on a structure or incorporated into a bedtime or bathtime routine. Accessorising using personal items and favourite toys makes the space more inviting and familiar.

Why?

- A range of sensory inputs sparks curiosity and creativity, as sensory space users learn to associate different sensations with new ideas and concepts, expand their imagination and explore and experiment in a safe environment.
- It encourages movement and physical activity, supporting the development of fine and gross motor skills.
- It enhances focus and attention.
- It establishes and reinforces daily routines, providing a sense of stability and security.

DOI: 10.4324/9781003601364-4

- It fosters social skills and bonding, promoting cooperative play and positive interactions with parents, carers, family and friends.
- It offers a quiet, personal retreat with minimal distractions where the person can unwind and relax after a busy day.
- It promotes healthy sleep patterns by helping the person to settle before bedtime.

Sensory Zones in the Classroom

Purpose

Sensory zones increase space in the classroom and have many uses, from providing a retreat to creating immersive and engaging learning environments.

Why?

- Create immersive learning environments incorporating materials that support curriculum topics, stimulate curiosity, engage multiple senses and reinforce learning through interactive and hands-on activities, making the experience more stimulating, dynamic and effective.
- Support emotional regulation through a calming environment for students to regulate their emotions and reduce anxiety.
- A sensory zone in the classroom fosters creativity and exploration.
- It creates an inclusive environment catering to diverse sensory needs.
- It increases space for dedicated activities or breakaway groups.
- It minimises the distractions of a busy classroom by creating a controlled environment, helping to improve focus and attention as students can better manage sensory input.
- It offers a designated area for students to take sensory breaks, helping them return to tasks refreshed and focused.
- It promotes group activities accommodating multiple students at once, encouraging social interaction, cooperation and collaboration.
- It provides behavioural support through a calming environment – a retreat or personal space that meets sensory needs to help children and teenagers manage their emotions and reduce anxiety.

Sensory Spaces for People with Dementia

By incorporating sensory spaces into adult environments, individuals can experience improved mental and physical wellbeing, enhanced focus and a greater sense of relaxation and comfort.

Setting up sensory spaces for people with dementia involves unique considerations tailored to each person's specific needs and preferences and can greatly enhance their wellbeing and quality of life. They can be set up in a range of places, such as the following:

- an activity room, to facilitate group activities or arts and crafts activities;
- a communal living room/day room, to serve as a social and interactive space where residents can participate in sensory activities;
- a dining room, as some people may prefer a personal space to eat alone;
- a garden area, to connect with nature;
- a multisensory room, to support therapeutic activities and sensory-based interventions;
- observation windows;
- an outdoor patio, to enjoy fresh air, the seasons and the weather;
- the resident's bedroom; or
- an allocated quiet room.

Purpose

- A sensory room can aid pain management through sensory activities that soothe and distract.
- It creates a supportive and enriching environment that enhances wellbeing and quality of life.
- It encourages social engagement and connection in shared sensory spaces, fostering community and togetherness.
- It enhances and enriches daily lives.
- It promotes cognitive function and stimulates creativity and imaginative thinking through sensory-rich environments.
- It provides emotional and physical comfort.
- It provides a designated area for sensory breaks, allowing individuals to recharge and refocus during the day.
- It promotes social interaction through shared spaces.
- It stimulates memories.

Considerations

When setting up sensory zones, ensure they are calming and supportive. Steps to do this might include the following:

- Keep it simple – less is more. Control sensory input with soft lighting, quiet sounds and calming scents.

- Incorporate familiar objects with new ones to provide elements of familiarity and evoke positive responses.
- Personalise the space to individual preferences.
- Ensure the environment is safe, accessible and hazard free with caregiver support to ensure the safe and effective use of the space.
- Monitor reactions and observe the person's responses, adjusting the environment as needed to ensure mental wellbeing.
- Involve the person, their caregivers and families in creating the space.

Suggested Themes

- **Culture:** Explore culture**,** traditional art, crafts, music and food. If partaking in activities, ensure they are achievable and provide a sense of accomplishment.
- **Festivals and celebrations:** Set up sensory areas themed around Christmas, Easter or awareness days.
- **Nature:** Reflect the season in the decor using colours, plants, scents and elements; play calming soundscapes.
- **Nostalgia:** Creating a vintage-themed sensory space for adults with dementia can evoke memories, providing nostalgia and comfort, enhancing social interaction if using a shared sensory space and building confidence among participants. Incorporate vintage decor, antiques, retro furniture, accessories or classic artwork or vintage posters. Use items from the person's past – old photographs, favourite books or personal mementos – to create a memory box. Play music from their era. Some people may enjoy listening to recordings of family or friends sharing stories or messages. Explore a specific decade (eg, the 1950s, 1960s, 1970s or 1980s) or a theme such as 'Washing Day', gathering representative items and decor. Source props from charity shops and car boot sales.
- **Relaxation:** An observation window and a comfortable blanket can reduce anxiety and agitation and provide emotional comfort. Offer the use of a sensory cushion or apron with different textures of fabric, buttons, ribbons and other objects to manipulate, to promote relaxation.

Sensory Zones for Adults with Learning Disabilities

Set up safe, supportive, sensory spaces for adults with learning disabilities by providing a tailored environment for promoting sensory integration and managing sensory regulation, thus building independence. This will enhance focus and attention, making it easier for individuals to engage in activities and tasks. Interactive sensory activities stimulate cognition and motor skill development.

Create sensory zones to incorporate activities that invite social interaction, helping to build increased confidence and self-esteem. Examples include 'All About Me' boxes, arts and crafts, board games, cooking, dance, gardening, group discussions, interactive technology, meditation and mindfulness, music, nature, photography, puzzles, reading, relaxation, sensory exploration, sensory stories, singing and themed days (eg, festivals, holidays and special events).

Sensory Spaces for You

This book may have inspired you to set up a sensory space in your home. The principles remain the same. Your space may cater to your personal interests and hobbies, such as reading, writing, meditating or creative pursuits. Bring sensory elements into your office space to create a more welcoming environment with focus aids, ergonomic chairs, noise-cancelling headphones, desk organisers and task lighting. Enhance using scented potted plants. Create a sensory nook in your garden.

The final part of this book, 'Sensory Zones', provides practical examples of setting up sensory spaces, whether for a child/teenager/adult at home, students in a classroom, persons with dementia, adults with learning disabilities or yourself!

Part 5

SENSORY ZONES

This part of the book provides practical examples of sensory zones that are easily replicated and adapted, whether in the home, school or other setting.

To make the experience effective and engaging, define the purpose of your zone. To guide its design and setup, consider whether it is an area for immersive learning, play, reading or relaxation. This will help you decide which type of structure to use. Create a balance between stimulating zones (eg, play area) and calming zones (eg, quiet corner) to cater to different needs.

Plan the layout to ensure smooth transitions between zones and avoid overcrowding.

Accessorise using props and sensory elements. Involve sensory space users in creating the space.

Keep it organised using storage solutions such as bins, shelves and baskets.

Regularly update your sensory zone theme to keep it appealing and engaging.

DOI: 10.4324/9781003601364-5

The Senses: Auditory Zone

Set up a designated space to promote active listening and sound discrimination and explore sound, enabling the sensory space user to focus with minimal distractions.

Stimulate the auditory system by presenting a range of familiar and unfamiliar sounds at varying volumes and in different locations to promote tracking. Play musical instruments; blow party blowers; hum; whisper; make gentle clicking sounds using your tongue for the listener to copy. Listen to the sounds of nature and bubbles pop; play sound bingo.

Theme listening games – for example, 'Animals' or 'Transport'. Experiment with volume and use of headphones for a personal experience. Explore audiobooks and different genres of music, noting individual preferences to calming/alerting music and diverse styles: grinding, hushed, monotonous, musical, intermittent, rhythmic, mellow or percussive.

Sound Effects

Using sound effects breathes life into learning and sensory stories in particular for an interactive and immersive experience.

Teaching people to produce sound using everyday items is a creative way to engage their senses, enhance cognitive skills and encourage them to explore the world around them through sound. Start with simple sounds – for example, pouring dried rice or beans into a metal bowl to recreate the sound of rain or hail.

https://sound-effects.bbcrewind.co.uk/ has over 16,000 free sound effects. These can be recorded onto sound buttons or played through a portable Bluetooth speaker.

Richard Hirstwood, director of **Hirstwood Training Ltd**, shares his ideas for using small portable Bluetooth speakers to offer auditory stimulation and vibration feedback.

Using Portable Bluetooth Speakers as a Sensory Tool

Richard Hirstwood

- Place the Bluetooth speaker inside a soft carwash mitten to soften vibrations, making it more comfortable for tactile exploration.
- Pair the speaker with a touch sound app such as ThumbJam on the iPad to promote cause-and-effect learning through sound and vibration.
- Use the speaker's vibration under a lightweight blanket to encourage learners to feel sound through different textures.
- Play slow, rhythmic sounds or soft music while the speaker is placed on a resonance board to amplify vibrations for sensory feedback.
- Position the speaker near the learner's hand or foot to let them feel subtle vibrations, supporting engagement and awareness of sound through touch.

The Senses: Gustatory Zone

Our sense of smell is linked with memory and emotions. Exploring smells helps individuals to understand the world around them. Create a space for exploring a wide range of different tastes and textures: bitter, bland, buttery, caramelised, carbonated, cheesy, chewy, chocolatey, citrusy, coarse, creamy, crispy, crumbly, crunchy, delicate, earthy, effervescent, fibrous, fiery, fizzy, flaky, floral, floury, foamy, fruity, garlicky, gingery, grainy, granular, gritty, herbal, honeyed, icy, juicy, lemony, malty, metallic, minty, moist, mushy, oily, oniony, peppery, pickled, plummy, powdery, pungent, refreshing, ripe, rubbery, salty, savoury, smoky, smooth, soggy, sour, spiced, spicy, spongy, squidgy, squishy, starchy, sweet, syrup, tangy, tart, velvety, vinegary, zesty and zingy.

Ensure individuals explore tastes at their own pace. Initial explorations could be through touch and smell. The next step is to present a tiny touch to the lips, progressing to a morsel or a drop in the mouth, a small spoonful and then building up to a full bite.

Play 'Guess the Taste' games.

The Senses: Olfactory Zone

Our sense of smell is linked with memory and emotions and helps individuals understand the world around them. Explore individual scents or focus on groups of smells (eg, citrus, fresh, fragrant, floral, fruity or woody).

- **Scent stations:** Place herbs and spices, fruits, vegetables, scented non-toxic plants and flowers, essential oils, scented creams and soaps and potpourri into small containers or bags. Label them to promote literacy skills. Alternatively, place items in the compartments of a paint palette or cupcake tray for exploration. Theme smells by colour – for example, a yellow-themed tray could include grated lemon zest, sweetcorn, bananas, raw potato, edible flowers such as sunflowers and marigolds, spices such as turmeric and cumin, yellow split peas and lentils.
- **Guided exploration:** Encourage the person to describe the smells. Have they smelled this before? Can they describe the smell? Does it evoke memories?
- **Craft activities:** Enliven craft activities by adding a few drops of essential oil, fresh herbs or dried spices to mouldables or mixing them into paint.
- **Scent-matching games:** Combine scents with images for the person to match.
- **Storytime:** Incorporate olfactory elements into storytelling.
- **Clean-up:** Clean up after the sensory exploration, making sure to clean the zone thoroughly to avoid any lingering scents or residue.

Corinna Laurie is the clinical lead occupational therapist at the **National Autistic Society** and author of *Sensory and Motor Strategies* (3rd Edition, Jessica Kingsley Publishers). Here Corinna shares her tips for using aromatherapy within sensory spaces.

Using Aromatherapy within Sensory Spaces

Corinna Laurie

Aromatherapy can be used throughout the day to help students feel calm, increase focus and assist regulation.

Oils should be diluted and used following relevant precautions and should respect the smell sensitivities of all students:

- Lavender and jasmine can help reduce stress and anxiety.
- Peppermint and lemon can promote focus and motivation.
- Sweet orange is uplifting.
- Geranium is balancing.
- Camomile is calming.

Keyring diffusers are a wonderful way to carry scents around to support throughout the day. Along with diffusers and spray bottles, pulse point roll-ons, nasal inhalers and a few drops placed on a towelling wrist band or handkerchief are easy ways for students to access the required scent.

The Senses: Tactile Zone

Explore items that provide good sensory feedback with a range of textures: bristly, bobbled, bubbly, bumpy, bushy, carved, coarse, corrugated, carved, downy, dry, elastic, feathery, fleecy, fluffy, foamy, gravelly, gritty, grainy, gooey, hard, hairy, icy, mushy, padded, pitted, pleated, pliable, prickly, puffy, ribbed, ridged, rough, rubbery, runny, sandy, silky, slimy, slippery, smooth, soapy, soft, spongy, springy, viscous, velvety, warm, wet and woolly.

Set up tactile art and crafts activities: explore paints, glitter glues, foamy soap/shaving cream, clay, sand, wood shavings, shredded paper, water, mouldables and textured fabrics.

Provide hand fidget toys; offer a blanket wrap; massage with or without cream; and explore the use of body brushes.

Explore dried foods such as lentils, pasta, pulses and rice.

Create sensory touch stations.

- **Tactile artworks:**
    - Create textured sculpture panels or wall-mounted shapes or reliefs using materials such as corrugated cardboard, fabric scraps, padded foam or shimmering cellophane. Shapes can represent abstract swirls, sunbursts or simple nature themes (eg, leaves and waves).
    - Use velvet, satin, sequins and foil-printed fabric to create high-contrast, textured collages on a board. Arrange in bold patterns. Provide magnifying glasses for close-up exploration of textures
    - Build layered 'artscapes' with bubble wrap, foil trays and padded contours. Illuminate from underneath using LED lights.
    - Arrange 3D shapes, buttons, curled ribbons, feathers, pompoms or nature items inside deep display frames.

The Senses: Visual Zone

Stimulate the sense of sight by creating a sensory space accessorised using vibrant colours, interesting artworks and items to track and locate.

Here are some activities to explore:

- **Bubbles, bubble tubes or lava lamps:** Use as a calming focal point. Watch bubbles rise or lava wax flow while relaxing music plays. Liquid motion timers or rotating projection wheels draw the eye and invite calm visual tracking.
- **Coloured lenses or overlays:** Invite learners to look through coloured acrylic sheets or overlays. Rotate them slowly in front of a torch to bathe the space in changing colours.
- **Foil curtain exploration:** Hang a foil curtain in a doorway or frame. Invite learners to watch it shimmer and sway or explore it through gentle touch, combining visual and tactile stimulation.
- **Glow ball rolling:** Roll soft glow-in-the-dark balls back and forth in a darkened space. Watch for eye movement or anticipation and practise turn taking.
- **Light-reflective mobiles:** Mobiles made of mirrored card, translucent coloured plastic or metallic shapes will move gently in air. Hang near windows to catch and scatter light.
- **Light tracking with torches:** Slowly move a torchlight across the wall or across soft materials such as silver foil or sheer fabric. Encourage eye tracking or head turning in response to light.
- **Light-up sensory bags:** Fill clear zipped pouches with gel, glitter or transparent items and place an LED strip beneath. Gently move the bag to explore changes in colour and shimmer.
- **Projected visuals:** Use a simple projector to display slow, looping images, floating shapes, rippling water or coloured patterns onto a wall or ceiling, or inside a tent.
- **Shadow shapes:** Use torchlight to cast large, clear shadow shapes on the wall. Explore moving cardboard cutouts (animals, people, simple symbols) across the light and narrate what is happening.
- **Spinning sensory objects:** Offer slow-turning visual toys such as peg spinners, slow-motion handheld light toys or battery-powered spinning tops with light-up features.

Creativity Zone: Arts

Art promotes fine motor skills, decision making about colour and design and visual-spatial reasoning. Set up a space for people to be free flowing with their creations; explore and create patterns, shapes and textures using a variety of tools and mark-making materials.

Theme your art zone, daily or weekly. Explore the following:

- **Media:** Charcoal, clay, crayons, paint (watercolour, gouache, acrylic), pastels, pens, pencils.
- **Activities:** Collage, cross-hatching, etching, engraving, fresco, fingertip and handprint art, impasto, leaf rubbings, lines, montage, mural, mosaic, printing, sketching and stippling.
- **Genres:** Romanesque, Gothic, Renaissance, Baroque, Neoclassicism, Romanticism, Realism, Impressionism, Art Nouveau, Expressionism, Cubism, Surrealism, Pop Art.
- **Colours:** Monochrome, pigment, tint, and tone. Experiment with multiple colours using a rainbow theme or focus on individual colours. Learn colour theory by mixing primary colours to make secondary colours, using palettes or Ziploc bags for a mess-free option.

Mix coffee grounds into brown paint or grass to green paint to add texture.

Meiry Geraldo is the mother of an autistic adult, a music therapist and founder of **GALERIA AUT**, an organisation in Brazil that creates a virtual space providing information on and sharing the art of autistic people. Meiry is passionate about art as a tool for people to express themselves and connect with the world around them.

Art as a Bridge to Communication and Expression

Meiry Geraldo

Art supports personal and creative development and fosters new skills. Providing opportunities for people with disabilities to 'experience art' is the beginning of something that often cannot be expressed in words. Their artwork reflects the sensory perceptions of the world, giving them a voice.

Here are five tips for artistic practice to build a relationship with art.

Observation

Observe how the person interacts with the art. How do they react to different styles, colours or shapes? What generates the most interest – painting, drawing, making collages, sculpting or music?

Praise

Recognise and celebrate. Praise encourages the artist and can increase motivation and artistic productivity.

Work Environment

Organise a space that stimulates creativity, minimises distractions and provides the necessary resources for artistic practice.

Step by Step

Set small, achievable goals that help promote confidence and competence in developing new skills. Remember that art goes far beyond aesthetics: every form of expression must be valued.

Routine and Exposure

Establish regular routines for artistic practice. This can solidify positive habits and enhance creative flow. If possible, create a continuous cycle of presenting works of art – whether for family, friends, at school or in public spaces. This will increase the artist's confidence and pleasure. Shows and exhibition spaces enable artists to recognise their form of expression and value their work, in addition to providing the public with greater understanding about autism, as the artwork facilitates social inclusion. By celebrating the art of our artists through exhibitions, we embrace the auspicious human experience and what it represents. Art has the power to unite, communicate and, above all, enrich the lives of all of us.

Creativity Zone: Crafts

Crafting enables self-expression, develops fine motor skills, enhances focus and offers opportunities to practise patience. A craft zone provides a dedicated space for ongoing projects – ideal for larger-scale collaborations such as murals, 3D art, papier-mâché and tiles.

Craft zones can be themed by festivals and awareness days – examples include Christingles, Christmas cards and decorations, dough Diyas, St Bridget's Crosses, St Patrick's Day bell pepper shamrock printing and Remembrance Day sensory poppies.

Junk box crafts encourage the use of recycled materials, fostering creativity, developing problem-solving skills and promoting environmental awareness.

Provide a box containing craft supplies for open-ended activities such as making friendship bracelets, dough and pompoms. For set activities, place all the materials required to make the item inside a Ziploc bag to keep them organised and accessible.

Diversity Zone

Exploring diversity provides opportunities for people to learn, explore, experience and celebrate different cultures, festivals and traditions.

Setting Up a Holi-Themed Sensory Zone

To set up an immersive area that captures the vibrance of Holi, line the floor with a colourful rug or blanket and scatter cushions and beanbags of various textures. String lights and hang silk or paper flowers around the chosen sensory structure. Incorporate colourful sensory items such as baubles, tinsel, finger lights, glow sticks and feathers. Add fresh and dried Indian herbs and spices, bay leaves, cinnamon sticks, cardamom pods, coriander seeds, cumin seeds, curry leaves, ginger root, nigella seeds, nutmeg, poppy seeds, sesame seeds, tamarind and turmeric root. Include textured wallpaper samples, paint charts from your local DIY store and coloured material swatches from curtain, blind or haberdashery shops. Lightly spritz fabric with scents such as rose, jasmine, sandalwood or musk; or place unlit incense sticks in a cloth bag and hang from the ceiling of the structure. Provide a dressing-up box containing saris, dhotis, sparkly and silky materials and dress jewellery, along with a safety mirror for sensory space users to see their look.

For activity ideas, provide a tray of items – chickpeas, colourful craft sticks, pegs and pompoms – with tools to promote fine motor skills: Balti dishes, a colander, cups, measuring jugs, scoops and spoons. Provide ice cube trays, cardboard egg boxes and snack trays with compartments for sorting and categorising the items. Play Indian folk music and provide instruments such as finger cymbals, triangles, spinning hand drums and shakers to play along with the music. Record the sounds of a Holi festival – fireworks, popcorn popping and people celebrating – onto a sound button.

Movement Break Zone

Providing opportunities for a movement break is an important aspect of the SEN classroom, to help students regulate their sensory input. While most schools and settings have designated areas, outdoor equipment and sensory rooms, there are times when a student needs a few minutes to regulate but using these areas is not practical – for example, if you are about to transition to lunch; if the student is awaiting transport home at the end of the day; or if the sensory room is unavailable due to timetabling. In such cases, setting up a mini sensory regulation space in your classroom can be beneficial.

Lay a PE or yoga mat on the floor in a quiet corner of the classroom. Space allowing, a trampette can be an outlet for bursts of quick activity and a physio ball can be used for balance. Where space is limited, equip the corner with resistance bands or a hula hoop that can be stored away. Movement cards with pictures of simple exercises, such as jumping jacks and stretches, aid independent use; the rhymes 'Head Shoulders, Knees and Toes' and 'Sleeping Lions' or dancing are other suitable activities.

Music Zone

Music stimulates the brain, with a positive impact on emotional and cognitive development, and on creativity. It helps individuals develop a sense of rhythm, pitch and melody – essential components for musical literacy.

Ideas for Creating a Music Zone

- Explore different genres of music, focusing on one genre at a time (eg, blues, cabaret, classical, country and western, dance, folk, jazz, hip-hop, opera, R&B, rock, pop).
- Accessorise your space with music memorabilia and display posters of famous singers and musicians.
- Place a selection of instruments in your sensory area for open-ended sensory exploration. You may wish to focus on one group of instruments (eg, percussion: castanets, chime bars, claves, finger cymbals, triangles, guiro, maracas) or one type of instrument (eg, drum: bongos, cajon, conga drum, djembe drum, floor drum, snare drum, spinning hand drum, steel pan drum, tom-toms, and different drumsticks and beaters, such as rubber beaters, wooden beaters and felt beaters). Change the instruments daily or weekly.
- Explore light-up musical instruments and interactive musical toys.
- If you have a budget, set up a Soundbeam touch-free assisted music technology device.
- Make an instrument activity area. Set up your space with the items needed to make an instrument using craft materials (eg, an assortment of containers, dried rice, pulses and beans and Sellotape to make shakers).

Music Reference Bags

A music reference bag helps individuals make connections between objects and music tracks. Select physical items corresponding to specific songs – for example, a kaleidoscope to represent 'Spectrum' by Florence and the Machine. Arrange the music reference items on a tray and invite the person to choose their song. Regularly change the songs to keep the activity engaging.

For younger children, a nursery rhyme bag teaches rhythm, rhyme and language skills, and helps to build memory and attention skills. Give the bag a shake, invite the child to choose an item and then sing the corresponding rhyme, presenting the sensory item for exploration. To help the child associate the item with the song, start by placing two or three items on a tray, then gradually introduce more as you add to the songs.

Sensory Items Representing Nursery Rhymes

- 'Five Little Ducks': Rubber ducks, feathers.
- 'Hickory Dickory Dock': Toy mouse, small clock with movable hands.
- 'Humpty Dumpty': Egg shaker.
- 'Row, Row, Row Your Boat': Toy boat, blue fabric for water.
- 'The Wheels on the Bus': Toy bus, toy steering wheel, bicycle horn.
- 'Twinkle, Twinkle, Little Star': Shiny star cutouts, fairy lights.
- 'Hot Cross Buns': Cinnamon or raisins.
- 'Rain, Rain, Go Away': Rainmaker or water spray bottle and umbrella.
- 'Incy Wincy Spider': Fake spiders or web.
- 'Mary Had a Little Lamb': Wool or items of woollen clothing.
- 'Old MacDonald Had a Farm': A lump of turf, grass or soil, straw or hay.

Georgie Lockett and **Karen Nicholson**, creators of **Songs, Signs & Sounds**, are SEND music practitioners and certified sound therapists who provide inclusive musical experiences for young people with additional and complex needs. Here, Georgie and Karen share their ideas for exploring music through the senses.

Setting up a Sensory Space to Explore Music

Georgie Lockett and Karen Nicholson

Choose a simple theme (eg, a season), then set the scene using lighting, scents, interactive boards, videos, pre-recorded sounds and music.

When using instruments, provide sound makers that offer contrast – something to shake, bang, scrape, tap or strum – or focus on a group of sounds (eg, wooden/metallic).

Heading outdoors and making or finding instruments from natural resources (leaves, sticks, pinecones) is a fun activity. Take time to explore them properly. How do they feel – rough, smooth, cold, warm, prickly? What do they sound like? Bang, scrape and scratch them; bring them close to your ears; tap or drop them etc.

Explore chanting. Use a simple name and chant to feel the beat on bodies, wheelchairs, floor, seats or foot plates. Simply chant, 'What can we do?' a few times and then wait – look for vocal sounds and body movements that you can copy.

Use simple songs/melodies that explore contrast (fast/slow, stop/start, soft/prickly, loud/quiet). Give opportunities for independent spotlighting as well as playing as a group. Use a gathering drum to recall the group. Large scrunchies/elastic bands/parachutes are great to shake together or pass round with different sound makers attached.

Play Zone

A designated play space provides a safe and stimulating environment for children to explore, learn and socially interact, supporting their overall growth and wellbeing.

Debby Watson was a social worker before becoming a researcher at the **Norah Fry Centre for Disability Research, Bristol University,** for many years. More recently, she completed a doctoral study of playfulness in children with PMLD and worked for a disability charity.

Here, Debby shares her tips for setting up a sensory space and activity ideas to promote play with children with PMLD and complex needs.

Encouraging Playfulness in Children with PMLD

Debby Watson

Playfulness, although almost always present, can be fragile in children with PMLD. In addition, what sparks it in one child may not be sparked in another, meaning that these 'tips' are really aspects of the rewarding 'playfulness dance' that I have observed between the child and their individual needs, the play partner and the physical and emotional environment. These aspects are as follows:

- **Observation:** To really understand a child's playful 'style', a period of careful observation is invaluable, noting what lights the child up.
- **Circularity:** Playfulness flourishes if both partners are fully engaged and looking for cues from each other in a to-and-fro that is 'tuned in' and sensitive, and with the expectation of playfulness.
- **Opportunities:** Creating opportunities to be playful may involve lengthy preparation and positioning; or it may simply be a shared moment of fun in an otherwise mundane situation, such as a dropped cup at mealtimes.
- **Control:** A child will be actively involved in playfulness if they have some control over their environment – for example, being positioned so that they are able to knock down a tower of bricks. Active playfulness has been shown to lead to the child demonstrating more 'strengths', such as the ability to engage in eye contact.
- **Modelling:** Children with PMLD need to see or sense playfulness in order for it to be encouraged. Being near playful children and adults will make the environment feel conducive and comfortable.

Popular Play Activities for Children with PMLD

- Small, tactile things hidden in a bowl of beans or rice, such as a 'hairy' ball or a toy animal.
- Bells sewn on to a glove or wristband.
- A pop-up tent with sparkly objects hanging from it.
- Foil space blankets.
- A festival atmosphere created through music, lights and disco balls.
- Towers of bricks etc for the child to knock down.
- Opportunities to demonstrate the child's sense of humour. These will vary according to the individual, but examples could include the child:
  - deliberately putting a ball in the 'wrong' place in a helter-skelter game;
  - pressing a switch with a message on it over and over; or
  - pulling funny faces to make others laugh).
- A biscuit tin full of items to shake or feel.
- A picture book of favourite places and/or things.
- Blankets with holes in them for the child to feel fingers through.
- A water mister, gently sprayed on face or limbs.
- Funny hats, scarves etc to dress up in.
- Changes in speed – for example, being pushed faster or slower on a swing.
- Bubbles with fragrance.

Reading Zone

A reading zone requires minimal space. For young children, a vibrant space with tactile books and toys in easily accessible baskets or boxes is inviting.

Primary school-aged children can personalise their space using posters of book characters and enjoy comfortable seating options such as beanbags and floor cushions. Teenagers may prefer a modern look, with comfortable chairs, space for tablets and headphones for listening to audiobooks, and books organised on shelves.

A reading nook for adults could feature a cosy armchair or recliner, relaxed surroundings and a reading light to reduce eye strain. Adding a magnifier or large-print books can also be beneficial.

Adapt your space for people with intellectual disabilities by creating an accessible, sensory-friendly environment, with access to assistive technology, e-readers with text-to-speech and a range of reading materials, including sensory stories.

Jennifer Abbanat, the founder and owner of **Crow's Nest Advocacy & Consulting**, lives in Davis, California, USA and is a parent to three neurodiverse children. Jennifer made an under-the-table reading hammock for her daughter by taking two diagonally opposite corners of a large sheet, bringing them up from underneath the table and tying them onto the top of the table.

Tents are the perfect base for creating dedicated reading spaces. They are inviting, provide a sense of adventure and can be easily accessorised.

FIGURE Z.3 Jennifer's daughter reading in her under-the-table hammock.
Photograph by Jennifer Abbanat

Christy Townson, a SEN teacher from **Hillside Specialist School and College**, uses a pop-up dinosaur tent as a book nook. Furnished with cushions and beanbags, it is placed near the bookshelves, with a Tuff Tray with related activities nearby. Students enjoy 'reading for pleasure' time each day, taking turns to read or look at picture books in the tent.

At home, Christy also has a safari tent and a tipi her son and godson enjoy playing in.

FIGURE Z.4 Dinosaur reading tent.
Photograph by Christy Townson

FIGURE Z.5 Reading in the safari tent.
Photograph by Christy Townson

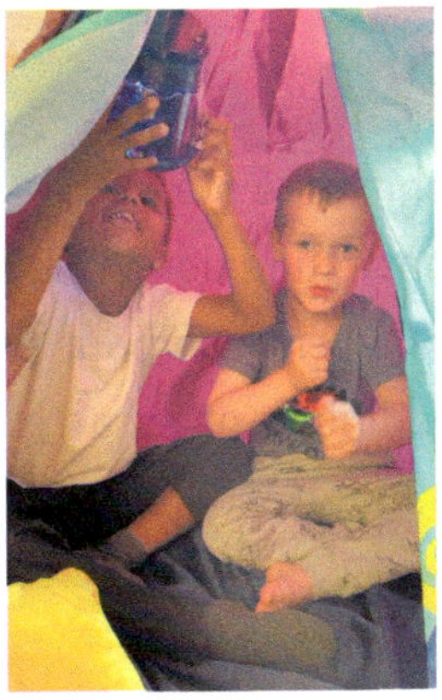

FIGURE Z.6 Exploring in the tipi.
Photograph by Christy Townson

Dr Sarah Moseley is an author, trainer and consultant specialising in literacy, inclusion and empowering neurodiverse learners. Sarah explains how setting up a reading tent encourages and promotes literacy by providing a comfortable and inviting space with minimal distractions to enjoy exploring books, encouraging independent reading, building literacy skills and affording opportunities for 'quiet time'.

Creating Engaging Spaces using Reading Tents to Promote Literacy

Dr Sarah Moseley

Reading tents and spaces provide learners with the message that reading is special and promote a lifelong love of literacy.

Some students may feel self-conscious reading in front of others, so a dedicated space enables them to read at their own pace and level.

Choosing the Right Tent

- For younger learners, a pop-up tent creates an enchanting reading nook.
- For older learners, a larger tent, wigwam or canopy attached to the wall can form a cosy covered area.

Comfort and Accessibility

- Add pillows, beanbags and cushions to make the space inviting and comfortable.
- Reduce sensory overload by controlling light, sound and touch.
- Blackout tents provide a calming environment and minimise external distractions, making it easier to focus on reading or other activities.
- Tents can be used to project images, text and more, adding another layer of interactivity and engagement.

Diverse Reading Materials

- Stock the tent with a variety of books, including fiction, non-fiction, board books, sensory stories, story mats and more.
- Theme the books based on current learning topics.
- Include comics, annuals and interactive books, such as *Choose Your Own Adventure*, to cater to different interests.
- Provide a dictionary and thesaurus to encourage students to expand their vocabulary and understand synonyms and antonyms.
- Use visual aids such as story maps, character charts and plot diagrams to help students understand story structure.
- Incorporate sensory elements such as tactile books or interactive elements to engage different learning styles.
- Consider storytelling approaches such as sensory stories and story massage.
- Keep changing the books to keep the students engaged and interested.

Audiobooks

- Offer a Kindle or iPad with audiobooks to build focus, concentration and imagination.
- After reading, engage students in discussions about the story. Ask open-ended questions to promote critical thinking and understanding.
- Use 'book talk' sessions where students can share their thoughts and opinions about books they have read.

Interactive Storytelling

- Use story cubes to inspire students to create their own stories, enhancing their creativity and narrative skills.

- Organise regular read-aloud sessions where students can listen and discuss stories. This enhances their listening and comprehension skills.
- Encourage students to take turns reading aloud, which builds confidence and fluency.
- Encourage students to act out scenes from their favourite books. This brings the stories to life and helps with comprehension and retention.
- Incorporate games such as word searches, crossword puzzles and matching games that focus on vocabulary and spelling.
- Use flashcards for quick, fun vocabulary-building sessions.

Writing Activities

- Have a journal in the reading tent for students to write about the books they read and their favourite characters, or to create their own stories.
- Introduce book reviews as a writing exercise where students can express their opinions and improve their writing skills.
- Incorporate multisensory techniques into all aspects of emergent literacy to enhance engagement and understanding. Technology plays a pivotal role, offering tools such as speech-to-text software and visual aids that reduce barriers to writing. For students with significant physical or cognitive challenges, alternative pencils such as alphabet charts, eye-gaze technology and adapted keyboards provide essential access to the writing process. Learners can use alternative pencils to contribute to a collaborative story, participate in sensory storytelling with tactile and auditory elements and engage in roleplay activities that stimulate the imagination and narrative skills.

By integrating these strategies, you can create a supportive and stimulating literacy environment that caters to diverse learning needs, promotes independent reading and enhances overall literacy skills.

RE Zone

Tents hold significant importance in various cultures and religions. Recreate these to experience immersive learning experiences. Here are some examples:

- **Sukkot tent:** Sukkot is a Jewish festival marking when Moses led his people out of slavery in Egypt and giving thanks for a bountiful harvest. A traditional *sukkah* is a temporary structure built from wood, canvas and branches with an open roof to view the sky. The interior is decorated with bread, flowers and Jewish symbols, with garlands made of apples, gourds and pomegranates hanging from the roof.
- **Sioux tipi:** The tipi serves as a home and a sacred space for ceremonies and rituals. Tents are decorated with symbols signifying the connection between the people and the earth, emphasising the importance of living in harmony with nature.
- **Bible tents:** Many bible stories feature tents. For an RE lesson, we recreated the story of Abraham and Sarah being visited by three angels (Genesis 18:1-15) through roleplay. We used a parachute to simulate a tent, incorporating props to bring the narrative to life. One student dressed as Abraham, wearing a head scarf and a long coat, and carrying a tall (cardboard) staff. Another portrayed Sarah in her long linen robe (we used a sheet) and bracelets. Abraham sat in the tent while others entered one by one and were welcomed with a handshake and a wet wipe to clean their hands or feet, mirroring the hospitality shown by Abraham in the bible story. Each student was invited to smell, touch and/or taste a potato cake or triangle of toast and butter, and to rest on cushions or beanbags. This was repeated until all the class were sitting in the 'tent'. As each student entered the tent, we chanted the following poem:

  Abraham and his family lived in a tent.
  He welcomed visitors that came and went.
  He gave them water to clean their feet.
  Let them rest and gave them food to eat.

Roleplay Zone

Roleplay fosters creativity and empathy, and promotes communication and problem-solving skills in a safe, supportive environment. Providing a variety of props and costumes makes roleplay more engaging and realistic.

Encourage participants to think up scenarios or, for added structure, suggest a choice of scenarios. Integrate roleplay into literature, culture, history and other subjects to support, enhance and bring topics to life. Roleplay themes include fantasy, superheroes, fairytales or everyday life situations, such as a café, dental surgery, flower shop, grocery store, hair salon, home, ice-cream parlour, library, marketplace, garage, pet shop, post office, school, vets or zoo.

Gina Bale is the founder, creator and director of **Little Magic Train**, a multisensory playful resource that engages children through stories, illustrations, music and movement. Here, Gina shares her top tips for make-believe made easy.

Roleplay – Stepping into Imagination

Gina Bale

Create a Magical Atmosphere

Transform your space into a world of wonder. Use simple props, music and gestures to ignite everyone's imaginations. Bright scarves can become flowing rivers; cardboard boxes can become enchanted castles or space rockets. Everyday items can be a treasure of adventure. Your energy sets the tone. Be expressive, enthusiastic and open-hearted. Invite everyone into a magical world where anything is possible as you foster a sense of anticipation and excitement.

Encourage Active Participation

Engage everyone through movement, sounds and roleplay. They could stomp like a giant, roar like a lion or tiptoe like a teeny mouse. Physical involvement makes the adventure come alive, allowing children to connect through their senses. Invite them to create their unique sounds and actions. This sensory exploration nurtures creativity, builds confidence and fosters emotional expression in a safe, playful way.

Follow Their Lead

Allow their ideas to shape the adventure and remember, flexibility is key! If they imagine a dragon instead of a dog, embrace it and make it part of the story. By following their cues, you empower them to take ownership of their journey. This approach validates their ideas, fostering self-esteem and trust in their creativity. It also ensures every adventure is fresh, exciting and uniquely tailored for everyone.

Model the Fun

Dive into the adventure with enthusiasm and expression. Show them how to leap across imaginary rivers, make snow angels or hide from a hungry dinosaur. When you wholeheartedly embrace the magic, everyone feels safe to let go of their inhibitions and join in the adventure. Your role is to inspire by example. When they see you having fun, they will feel encouraged, confident and safe to do the same.

Celebrate Every Effort

Applaud every contribution, no matter how small. Whether an idea is whispered, shared with a roar or observed with wide-eyed wonder, each action is worthy of celebration. Positive reinforcement builds confidence and makes everyone feel valued. Create an inclusive environment where every effort is seen, heard and appreciated. This approach ensures a joyful space where everyone, regardless of ability, can shine.

Incorporate Storytelling

Weave stories into your setting that they can shape and explore. Start with a simple narrative: a journey to find a magical key or help a lost dinosaur. Let their ideas fill the gaps, turning a basic plot into a collaborative tale. Interactive multi-sensory storytelling develops language and listening skills, and fosters a sense of togetherness and shared purpose.

Use the Power of Music

Music can transform a moment into pure magic. Use it to set the mood, from soft melodies for quiet reflection to lively rhythms for jumping and dancing or dynamic beats for stomping. Invite children to create sounds using simple instruments or household objects. Music enhances sensory engagement and creates memories that resonate long after the adventure ends.

Create Moments of Calm

Amid the excitement, allow time for stillness and reflection. A moment to 'watch the stars' or 'listen to the forest' helps children regulate their emotions and develop mindfulness. These quieter moments balance the energy and encourage deeper connection to their imaginative world.

Science Zone

Spark interest in science by setting up a mini science lab where learners can explore scientific concepts, use equipment and conduct simple experiments. Suggested resources include scales for learning about weight and mass; microscopes and magnifying glasses for examining small objects and details up close; and measuring tools, such as barometers, callipers, pipettes, rulers, scales, stopwatches, and thermometers. Safety goggles and lab coats ensure a safe environment. Set up sensory stations for making Oobleck, dough, sensory snow and jelly crystals; or an experimental area for testing magnetic/non-magnetic items. Linking scientific investigations to current themes or topics (eg, pollution) further enriches the learning experience.

Exploring Light and Dark Using a Tent

Christy Townson, SEN teacher, Hillside Specialist School and College

I use tents with students when doing science experiments. I used a dark tent to look at 'dark' and 'light' using torches and explore shadows. For some students, completing the tasks on their own in the tent increased their concentration in that environment.

We also used the dark tent to think about nocturnal animals and their eyesight and habitat. We built an owl's nest and a fox's den, and the children explored 'animals in the dark' roleplay.

The Sensory Calendar

Mark festivals and celebrations, historical days and awareness days with themed sensory spaces. For example, a tent, awning, gazebo or sensory tunnel would be perfect for a Halloween-themed sensory space – plan and build it with your sensory space user(s) or set it up as a surprise for them.

Enter at your peril!

- **Choose a theme:** Haunted house, spooky castle, witch's lair or pumpkin patch.
- **Decorate:** Involve the sensory space user(s) in making orange/black and green bunting/paperchains, hanging bats, spider webs and shredded ripped net curtains.
- **Add eerie lighting:** Lay a pathway of LED tealights; string lights around the structure; place a variety of torches inside the tent (Dynamo, headtorch, finger lights, flashlights, and wind-up torches).
- **Add spooky sound effects:** Play spooky sound effects such as eerie music, cackling witches, howling wolves, ghosts wailing and flying bats recorded onto sound buttons. Provide an echo mic for recording spooky voices; create ghostly wails using Whirly Tubes. Include a basket of props to create sound effects: flap black leather gloves to recreate the sound of bats flying; snap celery or dried pasta to sound like skeleton bones; tap blocks with beaters to make footsteps; and twist polystyrene to create squeaking and creaking sounds.
- **Incorporate costumes:** Provide black material for making witch and wizard capes and craft materials to construct witch and wizard hats.
- **Mix potions:** Supply a cauldron and utensils for sensory space users to mix potions. Explore spices: allspice, caraway seeds, cardamom, cinnamon, cloves, juniper berries, nutmeg, peppercorns, mustard seeds, nigella seeds and onion powder all produce a Halloween-like odour.
- **Create a 'touch and feel' station:** Place items inside boxes and bags – a peeled tomato for an eyeball, a coconut skull, graveyard compost, chia seed slime and cooked spaghetti worms.
- **Set up a pumpkin decorating station:** Place an LED tealight inside your pumpkins to create an eerie glow inside your tent.
- **Enjoy a sensory story.**

FURTHER RESOURCES

@Sohoplace www.sohoplace.org

Abbanat, Jennifer. Crow's Nest Advocacy & Consulting. www.crowsnestadvocacy.com

Allen, Carol. Educational Inclusion Adviser. carol.allen.work@gmail.com

Allen, Tracey. Made for Little Feet. https://www.facebook.com/share/19qTrhQ8zh/

Bale, Gina. Little Magic Train. www.littlemagictrain.com

Barson, Chris. Positive About Autism. www.positiveaboutautism.co.uk

Blaker, Peter. Starfish. https://www.facebook.com/profile.php?id=100063579070101

Boren, Ryan. Stimpunks. www.stimpunks.org

Brister, Rosie. Sparkle Sensory Education. sparkle.sensory.education@gmail.com

Calverley, Dr Julie. NAC Wellbeing. www.nacwellbeing.org

Castor Church of England Primary School. www.castorschool.com

Cerebral Palsy Alliance Singapore School. www.cpas.org.sg/cpas-school

Cowpe-Stephens, Julie and Dillon, Helen. Simply Sensory Training and Support Ltd. www.simplysensorytraining.com

Edgar, Helen. Autistic Realms. www.autisticrealms.com

Ellel St John's Church of England Primary School. www.ellelstjohns.school

EQUALS. www.equals.co.uk

Fitzsimons, Jo. Flourish Specialist Education Services. www.flourishspecialisteducationservices.org.uk

Geraldo, Meiry. GALERIA AUT. www.galeriaaut.com.br

Goodwin, Jill. Artist and Researcher. www.jillgoodwin.uk

Grace, Dr Joanna. The Sensory Projects. www.thesensoryprojects.co.uk

Graham, Claire. Inclusion Un-Limited. www.inclusionunlimited.co.uk

Hall, Sarah. Willows Sensory Service. willowssensory@gmail.com

Hebden Green School. www.hebdengreen.cheshire.sch.uk

Hill, Caroline. Making SENse Creative. www.facebook.com/sensorycreativeMakingSENse

Hillside Specialist School and College. www.hillside.lancs.sch.uk

Hirstwood, Richard. Hirstwood Training. www.hirstwood.com

Imray, Peter. Director of Developments at EQUALS. www.peterimray.co.uk

Kingsweston and Claremont School. www.claremontbristol.org.uk

Lockett, Georgie and Nicholson, Karen. Songs, Signs and Sounds. https://www.songssignssounds.co.uk

Manor Green Primary School. www.mgprimary.co.uk

McCann, Lynn. Reachout ASC. www.reachoutasc.com

McCormack, Gwyn. Positive Eye. www.positiveeye.co.uk

McLean, Jane and Spencer, Ruth. Cheshire Dance. www.cheshiredance.org

Moseley, Dr Sarah. Author, Trainer and Consultant. www.drsarahmoseley.com

Murphy, Emma. Little Mama Murphy. www.littlemamamurphy.co.uk

NAC Wellbeing. www.nacwellbeing.org
National Autistic Society. www.autism.org.uk
Navin, Victoria. Rhyming Multisensory Stories. www.rhymingmultisensorystories.com
Pauley, Emma. People as Partners. www.peopleaspartners.com
Peak, Chris. The Apogee Project. www.theapogeeproject.com
Prestage, Katie. Sensory Soup. www.sensorysoup.co.uk
Pritchard, Tigger. Hybrid Keynote Speaker, Conference Presenter, Trainer and Consultant. www.tiggerpritchard.com
Ravenscliffe High School. www.ravenscliffe.calderdale.sch.uk
Riverside School. www.riversides.org.uk
Scottish Families Affected by Alcohol and Drugs. www.sfad.org.uk
St Giles' School. www.stgiles.school
Sundin, Claire. Embracing Arts. www.embracingarts.org.uk
Swift, Daniel, MBE. Concrete Youth. www.concreteyouth.co.uk
The Den Kit Company. www.thedenkitco.com
The Story Massage Programme. www.storymassage.co.uk
Vivo Care Choices. www.vivocarechoices.co.uk
Wainwright, Gerard. The Unsafe Swallow Project. https://www.youtube.com/playlist?list=PLeLob98zDDNjRFtONhp0lsgsjoSoC1tqv
Walker, AnnMarie. Dragonfly Counselling. www.dragonflycounsellingservice.co.uk
Wanna Dance. www.pmld-dance.org
Watson, Debby. Passport to Play. www.thesensoryprojects.co.uk/covid19-resources
Wells, Pete. www.sensorystoriespodcast.com and www.helpkidzlearn.com/products/inclusive-stories/features

White, Joe. Inclusive Teach. www.inclusiveteach.com

9781032989112